ROMANS AND BRITONS IN
NORTH-WEST ENGLAND

New and Revised Edition

Centre for North-West Regional Studies
University of Lancaster
1997

Frontispiece. Carlisle: miniature bust of a female personification of 'the spirit of Carlisle', shown wearing a mural crown. Such an object was probably placed on a household altar.

ROMANS AND BRITONS IN NORTH-WEST ENGLAND

David Shotter

Romans and Britons in North-West England
by David Shotter

This volume is the thirty-fourth in a series published by the Centre
for North-West Regional Studies at the University of Lancaster.
Details of other titles in the series which are available may be found
at the back of this volume.

Editorial Board: Elizabeth Roberts, David Shotter, Angus Winchester

Text Copyright © David Shotter, 1993, 1997

First Edition, 1993
Second Edition, 1997

Published by the Centre for North-West Regional Studies,
University of Lancaster

Designed and typeset by Carnegie Publishing Ltd,
Chatsworth Road, Lancaster LA1 4SL

Printed and bound in the UK by The Alden Press, Oxford

British Library Cataloguing-in-Publication Data
A CIP catalogue record for this book is available from the British
Library
ISBN 1–86220–029–7

Contents

List of Figures

List of Photographic Plates

Preface

I welcome the opportunity kindly provided by the Centre for North-West Regional Studies at Lancaster University to produce a revised edition of *Romans and Britons in North-West England*. Since its publication in 1993, much has happened – both through new excavations and discoveries, and through new interpretations of existing evidence. I hope, therefore, that the picture presented in this book – particularly in the revised chapters dealing with military history – has advanced our understanding of *how* the Romans conquered and occupied north-west England. It is still, however, as well to remember that there are large gaps in our knowledge, particularly with relation to the local populations both before and during the occupation. This new edition will have performed its function if it has communicated information about new ideas, and if it serves to stimulate further the quest for understanding of this significant period in the history of north-west England.

Acknowledgements

I am grateful to Peter Lee for the figures (1, 3–6 and 9), which he produced for the first edition; these are reproduced here with minor alterations; also to Richard Turner who produced the map and plan (respectively figures 7 and 8). My thanks are due too to a number of organisations and individuals who have allowed me to use photographs of which they own the copyright – Professor Barri Jones and Manunair (Plates 1, 9, 15, 20, 21, 22, 23, 30, 37, 39, 40, 42, 72); Dr Adrian Olivier and Lancaster University Archaeological Unit (Plates 58, 66, 67, 71, 73 and figure 8); Carlisle Archaeological Unit (Plate 79); The Grosvenor Museum at Chester (Plate 12); The Senhouse Museum Trust (Plates 43 and 55); Cheshire Museums Service (Plate 64); Dr Timothy Potter (Plate 38); Mr Alan King (Plate 81); also to Museums who have care of objects illustrated here – National Museum of Antiquities at Edinburgh (Plate 3); Carlisle Museum and Art Gallery (Plates 56, 62, 74); Lancaster City Museum and Art Gallery (Plates 14, 29 and 44); Brougham Castle Museum (Plate 46); Ribchester Roman Museum (Plate 57).

Finally, my thanks are due to Christine Wilkinson, of the Centre for North-West Regional Studies at Lancaster University, for her preparation of the manuscript.

Notes and Abbreviations

Note: The majority of the military sites discussed in this book have seen excavation over a long period of time, which has meant that all but a few items from the detailed references for individual sites have had, for reasons of space, to be omitted. However, extremely useful summaries and bibliographies for the military sites may be found in M. J. Jones, *Roman Fort-Defences to A.D. 117*, British Archaeological Reports No. 21 (Oxford 1975). In addition, the annual surveys entitled 'Roman Britain in 19 ...', contained first in *Journal of Roman Studies* and (since 1970) in *Britannia* provide on-going and up-to-the-minute summaries of current excavations. At the time of writing, several excavation reports and site studies are awaited or are actually in the press: Carlisle, The Lanes (M. R. McCarthy), Walton-le-Dale and Papcastle (A. C. H. Olivier), Kirkham and Ribchester (K. M. Buxton and C. Howard-Davis), Birdoswald (A. Wilmot).

Abbreviations

Arch. Ael.	*Archaeologia Aeliana*
Arch. Journ.	*Archaeological Journal*
BAR	*British Archaeological Reports*
CAJ	*Journal of the Chester Archaeological Society*
CW2	*Transactions of the Cumberland and Westmorland Antiquarian and Archaeological Society*
EE	*Ephemeris Epigraphica*
GMAJ	*Greater Manchester Archaeological Journal*
JRS	*Journal of Roman Studies*
MAB	*Manchester Archaeological Bulletin*
PSAS	*Proceedings of the Society of Antiquaries of Scotland*
RCHM	*Royal Commission on Historical Monuments, England: Westmorland* (London 1936)
RIB	*Roman Inscriptions of Britain*
RIC	*The Roman Imperial Coinage*
Scot. Arch. Forum	*Scottish Archaeological Forum*
SHA	*Scriptores Historiae Augustae*
YAJ	*Yorkshire Archaeological Journal*

Plate 1. The Tebay Gorge from the north. (*Photograph courtesy of Manunair*)

1. *Introduction*

The physical environment of north-west England presents marked contrasts, which over the years have played a large part in determining patterns of conquest, occupation and settlement. The mountains of the Lake District are bounded on three sides by coastal plain, and separated from the Pennines on the fourth side by the significant communications corridor consisting of the valleys of the rivers Eden and Lune. Initial Roman strategy took account of the difficulty of this terrain by arranging its domination through control of the Eden and Lune valleys, and of the Solway Plain. This was probably enhanced by a readiness to intervene by means of coastal landings of troops based at Chester.

Further south, a broad contrast obtains between the Pennine foothills in the east and the coastal plain in the west. This coastal plain is itself penetrated by the valleys and broad estuaries of the Dee, Mersey, Ribble, Wyre, Lune and Kent rivers, which flow from the hills and facilitate communications inland from the coast. Conquest here consisted primarily of control of these valleys and their interconnection by means of a road running from the north Midlands to Carlisle, via Middlewich, Wilderspool and Lancaster.

Obviously, the environment determined the nature of settlement – in ways that ranged from the broad shape of agricultural exploitation to matters such as the availability of timber and stone for building and raw materials for craftsmen. Clearly, there were factors which presented conditions different from those obtaining to-day – the changing nature of the coastline, forest cover, and climate; however, current evidence suggests that in general during the Roman period exploitation of the landscape was at an impressive level, though building on what already existed to the extent that it has become customary to talk less of the 'Roman occupation' but rather the 'Roman interlude'. Research

in the Ribble, Lune, Kent and Eden valleys has indicated the deliberate positioning of farms to employ both the arable soils of the valley floors and the grazing potential of the valley sides, as well as to avail themselves of the developing markets and systems of communication. Similarly, the siting of farms on the lower slopes of the Lake District hills enabled both arable and pastoral potential to be exploited. An added incentive to such siting is the fact, demonstrated by pollen analyses, that favourable climatic conditions probably permitted the growing of cereal crops to a greater altitude than would be contemplated to-day.

Forest clearance, already underway in the pre-Roman period, was obviously accelerated both by the enhanced demand for timber (for building and heating) and by the need for land for agricultural usage. Consequent soil erosion from higher levels will both have impoverished the land at higher altitudes and have improved fertility at lower levels. Such environmental changes, however, will have required an element of control; some forestry management will have been necessary in order to conserve timber supplies. Overall, whilst the Roman presence may have acted as a catalyst to development in some areas, in general it is probably more accurate to say that it thrived because of the economic vibrancy of the region as a whole. Just as was the case further south, exploitation of the northern environment went some way to providing the means of support for the Roman garrisons of occupation.

From this it comes as no surprise that north-west England contains a wealth of archaeological sites of all periods, from the prehistoric to the modern. The Roman period is no exception: legionary fortresses, auxiliary forts, fortlets, watch-towers and temporary marching-camps provide the evidence of the military occupation by the Romans, whilst civilian life is attested in small towns (*vici*), industrial sites, farmsteads and at least one major urban centre (Carlisle). Connecting such sites was a network of roads, some of whose routes can still be traced on the ground with relative ease.

However, whilst this abundance of sites has long been appreciated – except perhaps for those of an agricultural nature – work on understanding them properly has been relatively slow, since until the 1970s most excavations were restricted in size and scope. Although small-scale trenching can produce dramatic, even inspired, results, there is no doubt that in recent years the provision of enhanced financial resources and the formulation of research-designs has enabled work to progress faster and to some degree more systematically.

In the last two decades, we have seen large-scale excavations and survey-projects at sites all across the north-west; these have embraced major fort and *vicus* sites such as Chester, Northwich, Manchester, Ribchester, Kirkham, Lancaster, Watercrook, Ambleside, Papcastle, Ravenglass, Low Borrow Bridge, Old Penrith, Brougham, Bowness-on-Solway, Carlisle, Birdoswald and Bewcastle, as well as sites of the Cumberland Coast. Further, Roman sites have been examined which are apparently non-military in nature, such as Wilderspool, Wigan and Walton-le-Dale; so too have a number of rural sites, such as Cross Hill Farm (Penrith) and Maiden Castle-on-Stainmore. Other sites, which are strictly outside the geographical scope of this book – for example, Vindolanda and Housesteads – have yielded results with important implications for the understanding of north-western sites. As well as this, funds (both public and private) have been provided for aerial reconnaissance which has not only told us much about known sites, but also (particularly in the rural context) shown up large quantities of sites whose existence was not previously suspected.

At the same time, a good deal of work has been done on the recorded finds from north-western sites – the inscriptions, pottery, coins and coin-hoards – which has enabled our understanding of the history of the Roman occupation to be refined considerably. Yet it is as well to remember that still only a tiny percentage of the area covered by Roman sites has been sampled, and that we are therefore still in great danger of producing interpretations and hypotheses which are based upon small and unrepresentative samples, and which future work will show to have been untenable.

Inevitably, since it is threatened sites which attract funding, excavation has to take place not necessarily where we believe that problems will be solved, but where rescue threats exist. Recent excavations at Watercrook demonstrate the risks this may cause: that work was concerned principally with the civilian settlement (*vicus*), for that was where the rescue threat existed. However, we now know enough to realise that it can be dangerous to hypothesise about the chronology of a Roman fort on the basis of evidence which derives from its *vicus*. In other words, until a major internal fort building is stripped, our views on the fort itself remain largely in the field of conjecture.

Thus, although we can assert with confidence that knowledge has advanced considerably in recent years, there are still many fundamental gaps in that knowledge. Most north-western forts still lack a detailed chronology, and some even a basic chronology. There are major sites, such as Wigan, whose nature is still in doubt; there are areas in which concentrations of finds or simple logic suggest that sites still await discovery – such as Colne and Burnley in east Lancashire, or the Fylde, or again south Cumbria; in particular, questions are constantly put regarding possible Roman activity around Fleetwood, Barrow-in-Furness and the Cartmel peninsula.

Again, the place-names of only three Roman sites in the north-west are known for certain – Deva/Chester, Bremetennacum/Ribchester and Luguvallium/Carlisle; this shortcoming detracts from an understanding of both communications and patterns of garrison-disposition (see Appendix IV). We are accumulating knowledge about rural settlement, but it is certain that a large number of relatively ephemeral earth-work sites must have perished in the face of the plough, and with them substantial numbers of temporary marching-camps for the army on campaign. Such earth-work sites tend to survive well only on marginal land, not subject to plough-damage; this means that the pattern of *conquest*, as distinct from the pattern of *occupation*, remains hard to unravel. As to the towns, – so important a feature of Romanised life – Carlisle has yet to yield a plan of a single complete public building, whilst the smaller towns (*vici*) are known only in

fragments and pose considerable problems in chronological interpretation. Until we progress further on questions such as these, ignorance will continue to surround the most important question of all – how did Roman and native coalesce into a Romanised social and economic unity – assuming, of course, that they did?

Thus, whilst this book will attempt as coherent as possible a view of the 'Roman interlude' in north-west England, many of the views expressed here are necessarily hedged around with caution. Hopefully, therefore, this book is at one and the same time a progress-report and an indication of the major questions which are as yet unresolved, and which present serious challenges to the historians and archaeologists of the future.

2. Before the Romans

Too often, the prehistory of north-west England has been dismissed with inadequate and inaccurate judgements: backward and sparsely-populated are descriptions which have been frequently applied.[1] However, the gradual accumulation of evidence and the development of ideas based upon that evidence have begun to reveal a rather different picture. For example, the fact that the products of the Langdale axe-factories have been recognised in Europe offers a glimpse of the importance and sophistication of north-western craft and commerce in prehistory. Further, it is a significant shift in perception that has led to historians ceasing to regard the Roman conquest as representing dramatic cultural change in the north-west, but instead applying to it terms such as the 'Roman interlude', signifying that the Roman presence was but an episode in a longer continuum. Our understanding, however, continues to be hampered by the fact that we continue to lack a clear means of distinguishing chronologically or typologically between sites of the pre-Roman Iron Age and sites of the Roman period itself.[2]

As in other parts of Britain, the historian is of course faced with the complete absence of documentation contemporary with the pre-Roman period. Thus, an understanding of the political, social and economic imperatives of the north-west before the coming of the Romans has to be based to a considerable extent on the observations of Roman writers. How far they understood or even cared about the political geography of north-western England has to be open to considerable doubt. Our chief source is the Roman historian, Cornelius Tacitus,[3] a senator of the late first century A.D., who in his later years turned to writing: of course, the major reason for his interest in Britain was the fact that his father-in-law, Gnaeus Julius Agricola, was governor of the province between A.D. 77 and 83, and responsible for the formal annexation of northern Britain to the province. Although we might in these circumstances have expected Tacitus to have been well-informed, there is little evidence to suggest that he delved any more deeply into British culture and society than had earlier writers.[4]

As we shall see in chapter 3, Tacitus tells us that the Brigantes of northern England – the name means 'upland people' – constituted the most populous tribe in Britain; and presumably on the basis of Agricola's campaign in the north-west Tacitus knew of two dominant geographical features – estuaries and woods. However, his lack of real interest is demonstrated by the fact that at one stage he referred to Boudica as queen of the Brigantes. Elsewhere, Tacitus provides some information on political tensions amongst the Brigantes in his account of the quarrels between the queen, Cartimandua, and her husband, Venutius. Further, Tacitus implies tension between different groups in his description of Agricola's tactic of playing groups off against each other (see Appendix 1). Some substance is given to these rivalries by the fact that when the north was Romanised, the centre of the *civitas* (Romanised tribe) of the Brigantes lay at Aldborough in Yorkshire; third-century inscriptions indicate the existence of a *civitas* of the Carvetii in the north-west, and the Alexandrian geographer, Ptolemy, writing in the second century A.D., mentions the Setantii, who are commonly placed in the Fylde, but who could, it has been suggested, have occupied territory in south Cumbria.[5] Although, therefore, our evidence is lacking in precision, it does strongly suggest the existence of a number of different tribal influences or 'power blocs' in the north; other tribal names, such as Tectoverdi, Lopocares and Corionotatae, appear in north-east England. All of this may point to the 'federal' nature of Brigantian politics.

Plate 2. Warton Crag: Iron-Age Hill-fort.

The policy of Rome towards these northern groups will be explored in the next chapter, but does archaeological evidence offer any clues to the political geography of the north-west which the Romans will have faced?

In early prehistory, sites had been largely undefended; the development of enclosures – whether by ditches, stone walls or wooden palisades – suggests the emergence of new imperatives. Clearly, a dominant requirement was now the ability to protect ones livelihood from marauders – animal or human. Agricultural exploitation was developing in later prehistory, so that lowland areas were extensively farmed in arable and pastoral contexts and upland areas were devoted to the grazing of cattle and of sheep where there was security from such natural predators as wolves. By such exploitation, farmers might manage to hold their own at a subsistence level, or might assert leadership through their ability to produce a surplus which could be traded.

The development of a society classified on economic grounds clearly led to rivalries within small 'tribal' groups, and in a broader territorial sense between separate groups which came to be regarded as separate tribes. Seats of power can be recognised in the appearance of hillforts, although the lack of research as yet hampers our ability to relate all of these sites chronologically; nor is it clear how far these hillforts may have represented places of retreat in time of danger or sites of permanent habitation. Some were small with a single ditch for defence, whilst others were defended by a prominent position and by more complex defence systems. Such 'hierarchies' may point to a growingly complex socio-political structure within these groups.

In the north of the region is a group of hillforts, of which the most significant is Carrock Fell, whilst Castle Head, Skelmore Heads and the multivallate Warton Crag form another group in southern Cumbria. There are major sites in the Pennines, such as the

5

impressive Almondbury and Ingleborough, the latter sometimes canvassed as the elusive seat of Cartimandua. Further sites can be seen in Cheshire. These may between them represent centres of groups which exercised a major element of independence, but which owed an ultimate allegiance to Cartimandua.

Such developments were themselves catalysts to requirements; competitiveness will have led to the need to clear more land for cultivation and to acquire the tools with which to manage this. The point has been emphasised by the recognition – for example, at Carlisle – of signs of ploughed fields beneath some Roman military sites. Although it is not clear how far the north-west's deposits of iron ore were exploited in prehistory, clearly the metal-worker emerged as a major figure in later prehistory. The tribal warrior-leaders required weaponry and decorative metal-work befitting their status; they also needed to be able to fit out their horses, for, then as now, the ability to ride rather than walk was a sign of status. Just as the metal-worker produced the trappings of that status, so too he manufactured the tools necessary to acquire position in society.

Although the north-west has produced no evidence of coin-use in later prehistory, the acceleration of the production of tools, utensils and decorative objects in metal, stone, wood and pottery should leave us in no doubt that the commercial pace of life was increasing. Similarly such developments also demonstrate the emergence of techniques for the management and transportation of the necessary raw materials.

Thus, when the Romans arrived in north-west England, they will have discovered an area that had been farmed for many hundreds of years. Although some extensive forest-cover remained, that landscape will have been predominantly one of farms and fields, of trackways which gave access to fields and summer-grazing and linked neighbouring sites.

Similarly, the process of the development of hierarchies had already in all probability led to the identification of tribes or 'sub-groups' other than the Brigantes themselves. Such a growing complexity of political relationships could, of course, lead to confusion as the Romans tried to come to terms with such difficulties; ultimately, it seems, it provided that common catalyst to Roman success which is summed up in the instruction – 'Divide and Rule'.

Footnotes

In these footnotes modern authorities will be referred to in an abbreviated form – for example, 'Higham, 1986' – which will be expanded to a full reference in the bibliography. The 'anonymous' citations of the periodicals, *Journal of Roman Studies* (JRS) and *Britannia*, refer to the annual summaries of recent work, 'Roman Britain in 19 ...'.

1. For the clearest, recent accounts of the prehistory of the north-west, see Higham, 1986, 117–149 and Clare, 1988, 9–27.

2. See Haselgrove, 1997, 61–74.

3. The most expansive of Tacitus' accounts of Britain is to be found in his *Life of Agricola*; other important passages are to be found in both his *Histories* and his *Annals*. These are all readily accessible in translation in the Penguin Classics series – the *Life of Agricola* by H. Mattingly, the *Histories* by K. Wellesley and the *Annals* by M. Grant.

4. Such as Julius Caesar and Livy.

5. Higham, 1986, 147; see also Shotter, 1995

3. The Conquest of North-West England

The Roman conquest of Britain began in A.D. 43 under the emperor Claudius; by A.D. 59, the tribes of the south and the Midlands had been brought under control, and together with much of Wales formed the province of Britannia. In that year, the governor, Suetonius Paullinus, was embarking upon what he expected would be the final onslaught against the druidic centres on Anglesey, when he was stopped in his tracks by the rebellion of Boudica, queen of the Iceni. This rebellion was in large measure due to mismanagement by certain Roman officials, and highlighted the need to consolidate what had already been won.

The rebellion also threw into high relief the value of the treaty which the authorities had with Cartimandua, queen of the Brigantes. The existence of this treaty meant that Rome had little immediately to fear from the Brigantes, and Cartimandua early on gave evidence of her good faith by refusing to harbour the Catuvellaunian chieftain, Caratacus. After his original defeat by the armies of Claudius on the Medway, he had retreated through southern England and Wales, hoping that eventually victory would be his. The failure of this 'plan' finally brought him (vainly) to seek Cartimandua's protection. At the same time, however, the rebellion of the Iceni posed a warning of the potential fragility of such treaties as Rome enjoyed with Cartimandua.

As we have seen, the tribal territory of the Brigantes stretched from the north midlands into southern Scotland, excluding only the coastal strip of east Yorkshire, which belonged to the Parisi, a tribe whose cultural links were closest with the Iceni and Coritani further south. The precise tribal boundaries are not known, through the discovery in Dumfriesshire of a relief-carving of the Romanised tutelary deity, *Dea Brigantia*, may indicate their northward extent; indeed the positions of the so-called 'outpost forts' of Hadrian's Wall (Birrens, Netherby and Bewcastle) may be related to the pre-Roman borders of the tribe.

We have observed that culturally the Brigantes were a Bronze Age people, made up of arable farmers, pastoralists, horsebreeders and metal-workers. Their rulers were probably intrusive with affinities further south; the great bank and ditch structures at Stanwick (north Yorkshire), which eventually enclosed around 750 acres, are reminiscent of the enclosed areas of the Catuvellauni in the south, which Julius Caesar had referred to as *oppida*.

The passages of Tacitus which refer to Brigantian politics are far from clear in their meaning, and they have generated a considerable literature in recent years.[1] It is clear that Rome entered into some kind of alliance with a Brigantian queen/princess, named Cartimandua. It is not clear when this happened, but it might have been soon after the Claudian invasion in A.D. 43; for not only did the Romans not apparently have to worry about their northern flank as they turned towards Wales, but, as we have seen, the queen decided not to harbour the Catuvellaunian chieftain, Caratacus, when he sought refuge with her, but preferred (and presumably felt sufficiently strong) to hand him over to Rome.

In Roman eyes, her stature gained from this, as did her wealth and influence. What is less clear is the course of her relationship with Venutius, her husband at one stage, and described by Tacitus as second only to Caratacus as a warlord. It is evident that although Venutius was anti-Roman by disposition he was kept loyal to Rome so long as he was married to Cartimandua. We may assume, therefore, that in terms of Brigantian politics the virtue of the marriage was its effect in binding together factions within the tribe and thus allowing Cartimandua's writ to run throughout the tribal area.

It is evident, however, that the Brigantes had something of a reputation for fractiousness, and that the relationship between Cartimandua and Venutius was a tense one, which may have restricted overt manifestations of Venutius' hostility to Rome, but without ameliorating it in principle. Roman intervention in Brigantia was evidently necessary under at least two early governors – Didius Gallus (A.D. 52–57) and Vettius Bolanus (A.D. 69–71), although we should note the contrasting views on Bolanus of Tacitus who regards him as inactive, and the late first-century Roman poet, Statius, who implies fierce action during Bolanus' governorship.[2] Further, although this intervention persuaded Venutius to bide his time, it was certainly not easy action for Roman troops.

At some stage the relationship between the two Britons broke down, though it is hard on the basis of Tacitus' evidence to determine precisely when this happened. It would, however, not be unreasonable to suppose that it occurred around A.D. 57, and that it introduced into Brigantian politics a period of considerable uncertainty. There is no need to assume any kind of reconciliation between Cartimandua and Venutius after A.D. 57; indeed her marriage to her former husband's armour-bearer, Vellocatus, at some point between A.D. 57 and 69 argues strongly against it.

These events had the effect of turning the client-kingdom into an unstable and potentially hostile neighbour. Skirmishing between the factions of Venutius and Cartimandua is explicitly confirmed by Tacitus, and this could well have continued over several years and included both 'civil' strife, manoeuvres such as the kidnapping of Venutius' relations, and the introduction of external forces in support of Venutius. These were contexts in which it would have been appropriate to introduce Roman arms; although Tacitus' accounts are, as often, aggravatingly vague in terms of topography and chronology, it is clear that more than one Roman engagement was involved. These disturbances culminated in Venutius taking advantage of the Roman civil war in A.D. 69 and putting so much pressure on Cartimandua that the Roman forces could do no more than rescue her, leaving Venutius in control of the tribe and thus from the Roman point of view a potentially dangerous situation which would require urgent action as soon as circumstances allowed.

The locations of their respective seats of power are hard to pinpoint: various hillforts,

Plate 3. Romanised personification of *Brigantia*, the tutelary deity of the Brigantes. The carving was found at Birrens (Dumfriesshire), and is now in the National Museum of Antiquities at Edinburgh.

such as Ingleborough and Almondbury, have been canvassed for Cartimandua, though the most recent evidence from Almondbury would appear to place the period of its use well prior these events. Sir Ian Richmond[3] plausibly suggested that Cartimandua's ability to rule the tribe may have been based upon the wealth and power which were represented by the richly fertile land of the Vale of York: both York itself, whose name (Eboracum) is not of Roman origin, and Aldborough (the later Romanised tribal centre) have been proposed, but both have failed to produce the appropriate pre-Roman evidence. It has been suggested[4] more recently that Stanwick, which has frequently been proposed as Venutius' centre, may in fact have belonged to Cartimandua. The volume of Roman material present on the site, it is argued, is inconsistent with a centre which belonged to Rome's chief adversary in the region, though it may be suggested that in the fighting in A.D. 69 Venutius took the site, enlarged it and made it the centre from which he mounted his final resistance to the Roman advance under Petillius Cerialis after A.D. 71. If these arguments are reasonable, it would not be unsuitable to locate his original centre in or to the west of the Pennines, particularly since much of the albeit tentative evidence for Roman military activity in the pre-Flavian period is located in and to the west of the Pennines. Further, the help which Venutius was able to summon from outside may in this case have come from north Wales, which had still not been properly subdued.

It has been traditional to assume that the principal credit for subduing the Brigantes should lie with Gnaeus Julius Agricola (governor of the province from A.D. 77 to 83); but this has been largely due to the high profile of Agricola guaranteed by the writing of his son-in-law, Tacitus, and by our lack of other coherent information. More recently, however, an enhanced programme of excavation and greater refinement of techniques of interpretation have left traditional views looking at best simplistic, and, at the worst,

misleading. Ironically, the keys to alternative interpretations have been available in Tacitus' writings, though we have lacked the evidence to understand them fully. As we have already seen, however, Tacitus (in his *Annals* and *Histories*) mentions occasions in Nero's reign when military intervention into Brigantian territory had been necessary; further, in the *Life of Agricola*, he mentions campaigning under Quintus Petillius Cerialis in the early 70s when, it appears, the greater part of Brigantian territory was either conquered or fought over.[5]

As far as pre-Flavian (that is, Neronian) intervention in Brigantian territory is concerned, Tacitus' language does not allow us to see clearly the nature, scope or frequency of this. However, finds of contemporary copies of copper coins of Claudius' reign, which did not survive in circulation into the Flavian period, perhaps offer clues[6] (figure 1). As we have seen, it seems likely that Venutius' seat of power lay in the south-west of the tribal territory; there is evidence to suggest that 'jumping-off' points in the north Midlands, such as Templeborough (Rotherham), Littlechester, Wroxeter and Whitchurch,[7] may have been used to launch 'search-and-destroy' missions as early as Nero's reign. In part, these may have concerned themselves with enforcing a separation between tribesmen in north Wales and in Cheshire. This purpose, for example, may have lain behind a road which ran from Whitchurch to the river Dee at Farndon/Holt,[8] and from there to Chester.

Plate 4. Copies of *asses* of Claudius: the one on the right (from Barrow-in-Furness) is a particularly poor copy.

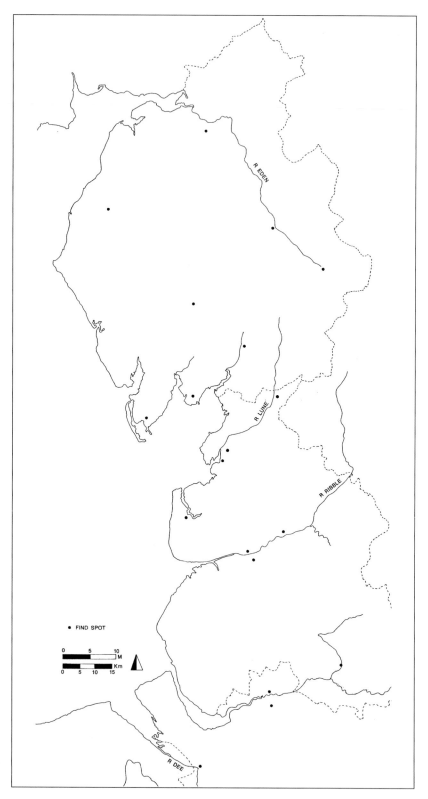

Figure 1.
Find-spots of
pre-Neronian
aes-coins.

There seems to be no doubt that there was a 'pre-fortress' auxiliary fort at Chester,[9] though its date of establishment and length of service are less clear. Its primary purpose, however, perhaps had more to do with north Wales than with north-west England; typologically, its use of the so-called 'box-rampart', in which a rampart of earth and turf was held in place by a complete enclosure of timbers, suggests connections with other sites, such as Rhyn Park (Oswestry),[10] in Welsh border-country. The distribution of 'Claudian copies' suggests that pre-Flavian military operations in north-west England employed the route the southern stretches of which are known as 'King Street'; this led through Middlewich, Wilderspool, and on to Walton-le-Dale and Lancaster (figure 2). At the same time troops may have been transported from the Dee-estuary, along the north-west coast, to be disembarked on river-estuaries such as the Mersey, Ribble, Lune and Kent, from where they made contact with the troops who had arrived overland. Tacitus describes the demoralising

effect of such tactics when employed later by Agricola in northern Scotland.[11] It remains as yet unclear whether such operations led to the establishment of forts, or whether their progress will have been marked by campaign-camps, which have proved to be much more vulnerable to plough-damage.

How far north such operations extended remains unclear, although finds of 'Claudian copies' in the Cartmel and Furness peninsulas suggest that the northern flank of Morecambe Bay, the putative territory of the Setantii, may have been covered. Further, recent evidence suggests the possibility at least that the operations may have extended to the Solway; finds of early material at Blennerhasset,[12] and the recent discovery of a large fort at Cummersdale (three miles south-west of Carlisle), point to early attempts to separate the Carvetii from their southern neighbours. Eventually, however, the task proved too difficult for the Roman army, particularly if it was trying to contain Brigantian factionalism from a distance. The Roman civil war of A.D. 69, as we have seen, proved for Venutius to

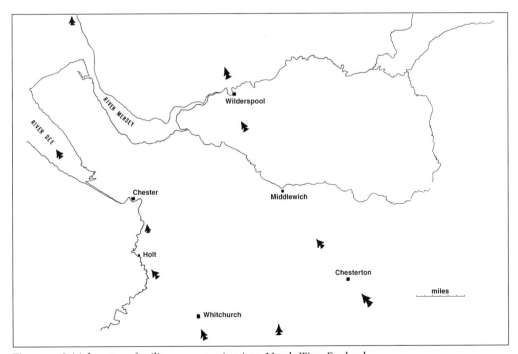

Figure 2. Initial routes of military penetration into North-West England

be an opportunity too good to miss, with the effect that Cartimandua was driven from power; full conquest of Brigantian territory was now inevitable – and urgent.

This task was thus a priority for Vespasian's new regime as soon as it had stabilised itself: two governors, Quintus Petillius Cerialis (the emperor's son-in-law and governor of the province from A.D. 71 to 74) and Gnaeus Julius Agricola (governor from A.D. 77 to 83) carried the limit of conquered territory from the north Midlands to the Moray Firth in north-east Scotland. It seems clear that Cerialis' work was both wide-ranging and successful, since his successor, Julius Frontinus (A.D. 74–77) was left free to resume the interrupted conquest of Wales, which was completed by Agricola in his first campaign at the tail-end of A.D. 77.

As we have seen, Tacitus, in his *Life of Agricola*, was somewhat grudging in his treatment of Cerialis' campaigns; the reason may be due to a desire not to appear to 'upstage' Agricola's work, though it may be the case that Tacitus was, in fact, less than enthusiastic over the achievements of a man who was probably less methodical than Agricola and who (more significantly), as brother-in-law of the emperor, Domitian, and probably as consul in A.D. 83, may have been closely involved in Agricola's recall from Britain in that year.[13] However, with greater refinements available in our methods of dating, we are able more confidently than previously to distinguish between the work of the two governors.

The method of operation during Cerialis' governorship, though not precisely described by Tacitus, may perhaps be inferred from an earlier comment[14] about this period when Agricola was commander of Legion XX *Valeria Victrix* during Cerialis' governorship. It appears that the forces were split up, and that, therefore, in all likelihood Cerialis operated on the eastern side of the Pennines with his old legion, Legion IX *Hispana*, whilst Agricola operated in the west (figure 3). It is usually assumed that during these operations the fortress of Legion IX was advanced from Lincoln to York, and that Cerialis actually defeated Venutius at Stanwick, and linked up with Agricola by crossing the Stainmore Pass where it is likely that because of their relationship

Plate 5. Rey Cross-on-Stainmore: Ramparts and entrance of marching-camp (seen from the interior).

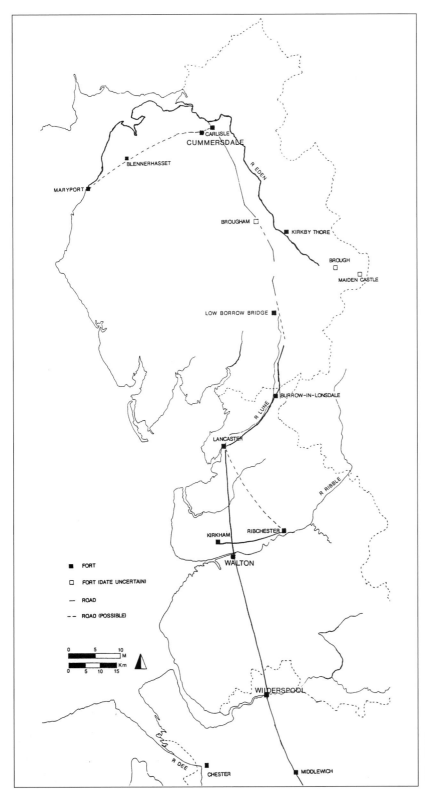

CARLISLE
CUMMERSDALE

BLENNERHASSET

MARYPORT

R EDEN

BROUGHAM □

KIRKBY THORE

BROUGH □

MAIDEN CASTLE □

LOW BORROW BRIDGE ■

BURROW-IN-LONSDALE

R LUNE

LANCASTER

R RIBBLE

KIRKHAM

RIBCHESTER

WALTON

■ FORT

□ FORT (DATE UNCERTAIN)

— ROAD

-- ROAD (POSSIBLE)

0   5   10
M
Km
0   5   10   15

WILDERSPOOL

R DEE

CHESTER

MIDDLEWICH

Figure 3.
Early Flavian
sites in North-
West England.

Plate 6. Ribchester: Timber corduroy, or rampart-base.

with the road, the temporary marching-camps such as Rey Cross and Crackenthorpe, were established by Cerialis.[15] The use of this route in the early Flavian period receives strong confirmation from dates recently established for timbers from the rampart-base of the earliest fort at Carlisle; these dates show that the timbers were felled at some stage during the winter of A.D. 71–72.[16] Confirmation of this date may be found in a significant group of pre-Flavian and early Flavian coins.

Other sites in north-west England belonging to Cerialis' governorship remain harder to locate with such certainty. Tacitus indicates that during Cerialis' period of office, Agricola, who was then commander of Legion XX, operated with a degree of independence. It is likely that Agricola mirrored his commander's basic strategy on the other side of the Pennines – that is, working to separate groups from each other and thus destroy tribal coherence, moving northwards to effect a junction with Cerialis presumably in the neighbourhood of Brougham. It is unlikely that Chester was the base for this operation, but rather that troops came northwards from bases further south – for example, at Littlechester, Wroxeter and Whitchurch – with a principal route of penetration, as before, adopting the line of King Street, through Middlewich, crossing the Mersey a little upstream of the later industrial site at Wilderspool, and from there making for Walton-le-Dale and Lancaster. It seems that from Lancaster, the Lune and Eden valleys provided a route to Carlisle, though the identity of sites established on this route *at this time* remains uncertain.

It seems likely, too, that, as before, troops were carried by sea to be disembarked at key points; one of these was almost certainly the Ribble estuary, where at Kirkham a campaign-camp appears to represent the first in a series of structures;[17] recent excavations recovered a very fine example of a *pilum murale*, one of a series of stakes which were inserted to make a fence on the top of the rampart of such a site. Dendrochronological evidence from Ribchester[18] suggests that the first in a long series of structures and modifications should be dated to this period also. It appears likely that the tactic of coastal landing was carried up as far north as the Solway; the fort at Blennerhasset, already mentioned, which at 8.4 acres, was one of the largest in Cumbria, seems to have been operational at this time, and modifications (albeit at an uncertain date) were made at Cummersdale. From this it seems that the early separation of the Carvetii, as with the Parisi in eastern Yorkshire, was actively pursued. It is worth bearing in mind that the complex collection of linear constructions with occasional watchtowers, which will be discussed below, remains largely undated, and thus could conceivably have been started at this early stage.

The truth, however, of Tacitus' statement concerning the wide-ranging and bloody nature of Cerialis' activities, and with it by

Plate 7. Carlisle: Coins of the Flavian period excavated at Annetwell Street.

implication their thoroughness and effectiveness, is borne out by two considerations. First, it is evident that Cerialis' successor, Julius Frontinus, was able to operate in north Wales with no fear of being 'stabbed in the back': and secondly, there is the fact that when, after the completion of the Welsh conquest, Agricola turned back to the north, he secured it in a single campaigning season.

Tacitus' account of Agricola's campaign against the Brigantes in A.D. 78[19] is unsatisfactory in the extreme if we wish to use it to determine Agricola's precise routes (figure 4). A number of 'shadowy clues' may, however, be put to work; first, it is evident that the campaign represented a twin advance on both sides of the Pennines – a point which has received some corroboration from the discovery in 1974 of a major Agricolan military site at Red House, near Corbridge.[20] Secondly, Tacitus seems to show that Agricola (perhaps reiterating Cerialis' policy) gained the co-operation of the various Brigantian groups by encircling them and thus separating and protecting them from their neighbours. This in its turn would suggest a concentration on the chief river-valleys, which effectively separated the defended sites on the high ground. Detail is, of course, lacking in our

knowledge of this, since whilst we can show a considerable number of hill-forts, few have been examined with a view to establishing whether or not their dating will tie them into this period. Thirdly, a general indication of topography is contained in Tacitus' remark about estuaries and woods, which applies very well to Lancashire in particular. Fourthly, we may infer from this, and from a remark which Tacitus makes about the joint use of fleet and troops in the later Scottish campaigns, that it remained Agricola's policy to disembark troops in the main estuaries and march them up the valleys where they could join with troops taking overland routes.

In the interval between Cerialis' and Agricola's campaigns, the legionary fortress at Chester had been commenced, and a piece of stamped lead waterpipe[21] indicates that the construction continued into Agricola's governorship; as a legionary base, Chester could now, therefore, become a starting-point for overland-operations in the north-west, and Agricola probably opened the route through Northwich, Manchester and Ribchester, joining the earlier route in the vicinity of Burrow-in-Lonsdale. It is likely, too, that Ribchester, in the first of a complex series of modifications, may have been re-orientated to face northwards. With the conquest of the north established, trans-Pennine routes assumed a heightened importance: that through Castleshaw,[22] which linked Chester with York, will have been built now – as also probably, further north, that from Corbridge to Carlisle, which was before long to become the frontier of Roman Britain.

A major problem in tracing Agricola's movements is that much of our evidence derives from sites which became permanent, and which therefore provide us with information about the long-term policing network for the area. Some of these may lack occupation from the Agricolan period because Agricolan sites were located near them rather than always providing the earliest levels on such sites of long-term occupation. It is possible in any case that some of the movements of the early Flavian period – or even earlier – were represented only by temporary marching-camps. Because such sites were by their nature occupied only for short periods, they leave little occupation-debris for dating; further, as earth-work sites, they are likely to have been substantially destroyed in areas subject to long-term ploughing, and are, therefore, often identifiable only by the most sophisticated survey-methods. Only when located on land of marginal agricultural value do such sites survive in visible form – as at Rey Cross (Stainmore), Mastiles Lane (Malham Moor), Brackenrigg and Troutbeck.[23] It is virtually impossible to place such sites into a specific model of conquest, though we have seen that there is some reason to place the Stainmore sequence of camps earlier than Agricola's governorship, even though we cannot regard this case as proved. It is further worth noting than none of the temporary camps so far identified in north-west England have entrance-ways which conform typologically with the distinctive Agricolan camps located in Scotland at such sites as Stracathro.[24]

Agricola's permanent forts contained timber buildings and were defended by ramparts of turf and clay laid on a foundation of logs (corduroy). The rampart was often sup-ported by a timber revetment or fence on the inside, though sometimes in earlier examples, as we have seen, by a complete box-like enclosing fence. Outside were ditches and other obstacles. At Watercrook,[25] for example (itself not an Agricolan site), between the first and second ditches was a palisade fence made probably of branches, and an earth and rubble bank. The rampart was pierced by double-carriageway gates with guard-towers, which led to a central range of buildings consisting of headquarters, granaries and commandant's house, whilst the rest of the area would be occupied largely by barracks and stables.

It should be noted that, whilst it is true that Agricola did not leave stone-built forts, those constructed of turf and timber were chronologically far more widespread than has sometimes been supposed, and therefore do not by themselves offer conclusive evidence of occupation in the Agricolan period.

Although the direction and extent of Agricola's single campaign in north-west England has always been a matter of considerable speculation, its speed suggests that much successful work had been achieved by his predecessors, and Tacitus' account indicates that Agricola was able to play 'sub-groups' of the north-western Brigantes off against each other; the removal of both Cartimandua and Venutius had evidently destroyed the coherence of the tribe. It seems unlikely that Agricola will have had time (and presumably did not need) to do more than to sweep northwards from Chester to Carlisle along a route which later came to represent the chief communications-artery through north-west England. This led along the foothills of the Pennines and then followed the lines of the rivers Lune and Eden. Control of these valleys and of the natural passes across the Pennines will have given Agricola an effective stranglehold on the region. It appears that for the time being at least the Lake District could be left largely unattended, and that it was not fully penetrated until later in the first and early in the second centuries A.D.

Considerable stretches of the main northward route survive in various forms; between Penrith and Carlisle, the modern A6 follows its route, whilst it can be picked out by minor roads between Manchester and Ribchester; between Ribchester and Burrow-in-Lonsdale, a particularly impressive stretch can be seen from Jeffry Hill (on Longridge Fell) as the road heads northwards to cross the river Hodder.[26] Further north, stretches of minor road reflect the original course near Burrow-in-Lonsdale, and a cylindrical stone now functioning as a parish boundary may be the surviving stump of an *in situ* milestone. South of Low Borrow Bridge, the road is impressively preserved on the eastern side of the Lune Valley, and a recent (1991) excavation at Orton has revealed its construction with a distinctive central spine of heavy cobbles. The road also survives in part as an earth work in Barbondale, with a complete milestone surviving at Middleton-in-Lonsdale, although not standing precisely at its original location.

Many of the sites relating to conquest have seen excavation and discussion over recent years; at Chester, a large number of excavations over the years have revealed buildings of many periods both inside and outside the legionary fortress.[27] Those of the 1970s on Abbey Green, for example, not only demonstrated the existence of a turf rampart, which clearly represents the primary phase of the fortress-defences, but also evidence beneath it of a 'box-rampart' which constituted the defences of the likely earlier auxiliary fort. From Chester, a road led to Northwich,[28] the intermediate point between Chester and Manchester; work in the late 1960s revealed elements of a turf-and-timber fort of the Flavian period on Castle Hill. This has subsequently been shown to have been partly overlain by another fort, probably of second-century date.

Excavation and observation over the years has established the layout of an auxiliary fort at Manchester on Castlefield (off Deansgate).[29] Recent excavations on the northern and western defences[30] have shown elements of the northern gateway, rampart and ditch-

system of a fort which evidently had two turf-and-timber phases, the earlier of which is regarded as of Agricolan date, the second late Flavian/Trajanic: the fort was evidently substantially enlarged around the middle of the second century, perhaps following the withdrawal from the Antonine Wall in *c*. A.D. 165. It is worth noting that outside the western ditches lay pits interpreted as a defensive feature known as *lilia*; a sharpened stake was inserted into each pit, with its point upturned, and the pit then covered with brushwood to provide an extremely hazardous 'man-trap'. A very fine example of this feature is to be seen to the north of the Antonine Wall, at Rough Castle.

North of Manchester, the situation becomes more complex; although a road runs northwards via Affetside to Ribchester, the third-century road-list, known as *The Antonine Itinerary*, indicates a route from Ribchester to Manchester which has an in-

Plate 8. Jeffry Hill (Longridge): Stretch of the Roman road between Ribchester and Burrow-in-Lonsdale (line arrowed on horizon).

Plate 9. Stainmore: Circular earthwork of the watchtower near The Punch Bowl Hotel. (*Photograph courtesy of Manunair*)

termediate site, named *Coccium*. This has usually been taken to be Wigan,[31] where many Roman finds have been made, and where in recent years excavations have revealed timber buildings with three phases of occupation, which have been placed between the early second and early third centuries. There is nothing in the present evidence to suggest either that these structures were of military origin or that they played any part in the original conquest of the northwest. If *Coccium* is indeed Wigan (and not another site between Manchester and Ribchester), then we should regard the route given in *The Antonine Itinerary* as of later significance when consolidation of the original conquest had resulted in a greater complexity of site-distribution (see below in chapter 4).

At Ribchester, the evidence points to a foundation at least as early as Cerialis' governorship; a good deal of the fort's area – approximately 30 per cent – has been lost to erosion by the river, but what remains provides evidence of fort-phases both of turf-and-timber construction and of stone-building. The excavated remains probably indicate re-orientation or realignment of the fort at some stage – perhaps during the first or second centuries A.D. – and this may be connected with a garrison-change; an early garrison of Asturian cavalry from Spain was probably redeployed on Hadrian's Wall early in the second century A.D., and later in that century Ribchester received a part of the large group of Sarmatian cavalry brought from the Danube by the emperor, Marcus Aurelius (A.D. 161–180).

Plate 10. Blackstone Edge (Rochdale): Paved Roman road climbing a gradient of sometimes 1 in 4.

Elements of the defences of the Ribchester forts have been observed in a number of recent excavations – a clay-and-turf rampart rested on a log base (known as a corduroy), and at one point it could be seen that the turves were approximately one foot square, and that each layer was interleaved with brushwood. The multi-phase ditches include three different types – a traditional V-shaped ditch, a 'Punic' ditch (with a near-vertical outer face), and a much shallower type which can still be seen as a feature in some of the fields near to the church.

As well as being placed on the north–south road, Ribchester lay on a road which ran along the north bank of the Ribble; this road ran to the north of Preston to Kirkham, and may then have turned north to the mouth of the river Wyre, perhaps terminating at a site which has possibly been lost off the coast near Fleetwood. It has long been held that this site may have been Ptolemy's *Portus Setantiorum*, and that the Setantii were a sub-

group of the Brigantes, living in or close to the Fylde. As we have seen, however, recent hypotheses have tended to locate the elusive Setantii (and presumably their *Portus*) on the northern side of Morecambe Bay.

Excavation (in 1994) on the last available area of the fort-site at Dowbridge (Kirkham) revealed a complex series of structures; the earliest, which may belong to Cerialis' governorship, appears to have been a campaign-camp; this seems to have been superseded by a watchtower which was in its turn replaced by an auxiliary fort. Although a clear chronology has proved difficult to establish, the watchtower may date to Agricola's governorship, and the fort to the period of reorganisation following the evacuation of Scotland in *c.* A.D. 87. This fort was maintained in operation at least until the middle of the second century A.D.

South of the Ribble at its confluence with the Darwen, lies Walton-le-Dale. Speculation about this site has been intense in the past, but recent excavations appear to have put beyond reasonable doubt the likelihood that the site was military in nature.[32] On the other hand, it has to be said that the buildings excavated do not resemble those of a conventional fort layout. Though of a large scale they would appear to be more consistent with a manufacture, storage and supply role.

A possibility, which remains to be fully considered, is that these buildings may have been preceded by a conventional fort dating back as early as the 60s and relating to the earliest intervention in the area; the river Ribble will have provided an excellent line for penetration and communication. This presumed early site at Walton-le-Dale would appear to have been abandoned by the early 70s, and the storage buildings were constructed only after an interval of inactivity at the site.

From both Ribchester and Manchester run trans-Pennine links: from Manchester a road runs across Saddleworth Moor, heading for York; there are forts along it at Castleshaw and Slack. At the former, there is a fortlet, which has timber buildings and which has been assumed to be Agricolan, and a smaller later fortlet inside[33] and partly contiguous with it. This later fortlet, which is assumed to have been Trajanic in date contained a rather strange collection of buildings consisting of a barrack-block, a courtyard building, a commander's house (with a bath-house),

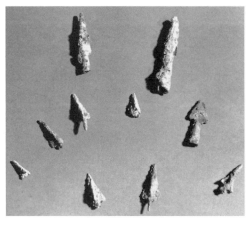

Plate 11. Roman weapon-heads (from Watercrook Roman fort).

latrines and a granary which was apparently larger than this fortlet would require. Both fortlets, each of which probably had two phases of construction, were contained within turf ramparts.

Another road heads from Manchester to Ilkley, though doubt continues to surround the relation to it of the paved surface which runs over Blackstone Edge; yet another leads south-eastwards towards Melandra[34] and Brough-on-Noe.[35] It is likely that the Ribble-Aire corridor[36] was supplied with a signalling system similar to that identified over Stainmore (see below). Indeed the existence of a small earthwork at Mellor Hill, above Ribchester, may be a fragment of it. It is further possible that a site of a similar nature may await discovery near Whalley, to judge from occasional finds of Roman material in the area, and the presence of an altar (probably to the God, Mars) in Whalley church[37] – that is, if this has not been transported from elsewhere.

The military road ran northwards from Ribchester to Burrow-in-Lonsdale:[38] the road itself is still impressively preserved over a number of stretches, although of the fort at Burrow virtually nothing can be seen. The fort, like many, is protected by a confluence of rivers – in this case, the Lune and the Leck Beck; it lies at a distance from the main north–south route which prompts the suggestion that it may not be the earliest military site in the area. Limited excavation has taken place, but on the whole tells us more of the later stages of the fort's development than of its initial phases, although it appears that at some stage reorientation occurred. A turf-and-timber phase was located and, although not certainly dated, it would not be inconsistent with an Agricolan beginning.

If that is so, then we can see Burrow as occupying a crucial position in the Lune Valley control system, since it looks in one direction to Low Borrow Bridge in the upper Lune gorge and in the other to Lancaster up to which point at least the river Lune was navigable.

Plate 12. Chester: Length of lead water-pipe, which is dated to A.D. 79 and bears Agricola's name. (*Photograph courtesy of the Grosvenor Museum, Chester*)

Plate 13. Lancaster: Clay-and-turf rampart of an early Flavian fort.

The fort site at Lancaster occupies, rather unusually, a hill-top position. Although it is clear that the sequence of structures, military and civilian, on Castle Hill is complex, we can now be certain of an Agricolan, or possibly earlier, beginning, both on ceramic and numismatic evidence.[39] In the grounds of the old vicarage, running east-west, was an especially well-preserved turf-and-clay rampart, surviving to a height of 1.3 metres. Since this rampart had timber buildings erected across it, we can only assume that later forts were larger, and that the rampart survived because the whole platform had been levelled up. Further, there was no sign of the Trajanic stone rampart to be inferred from a building-slab found in the Priory Church.[40] However, the discovery of a bevelled plinth course on a line that would take it only a few yards north of the clay-and-turf rampart suggests that on the north side at least the enlargement was not great. If this was the northern defence of the Agricolan fort, it is likely that the western defence of the same fort was located in western Vicarage Field in 1971. On the other hand, although an eastern gateway was found near the junction of Church Street and China Street, there was no evidence there of a turf-and-timber phase, suggesting that the eastern rampart of the Agricolan fort was a little higher up Castle Hill. It is also worth noting that at some stage before it went out of use, this turf rampart underwent a modification, possibly indicating a short break in occupation in the later Flavian period – a suggestion which would not be at variance with the numismatic record.[41]

A road running on the south bank of the Lune towards Burrow is certainly attested in the Hadrianic period by the fine milestone found at Caton. In addition, stretches of this road were observed in 1992 during pipeline-work in the Quernmore/Caton/Brookhouse area. The Lune Valley route joined the Rib-chester-Burrow road possibly at its crossing of the Wenning.[42] The upper Lune was pro-tected by the fort at Low Borrow Bridge (Tebay), the outline of which is still clearly preserved. Excavation of the site has been limited, and the dating evidence, although consistent with pre-Hadrianic activity, does not require a date as early as Agricolan. How-ever, it does not seem reasonable that Agri-cola did not establish a site in this area: thus either an Agricolan site awaits location or, rather like Lancaster and as suggested by Hildyard,[43] the Agricolan fort was a smaller one situated within and beneath the area of

Plate 14. Caton: Hadrianic milestone. The inscription reads: 'For the Emperor Caesar Trajan Hadrian Augustus, Chief Priest, with Tribunician Power, three times Consul, Father of his Country, from ... 4 miles'. (*Lancaster City Museum and Art Gallery*)

the later fort. The most recent excavations (approximately half a mile south of the fort) have revealed the road running south from the fort and part of the site-cemetery on its eastern side.

At Brougham, the north–south route joined with that coming across Stainmore. As has already been noted, it is usually held that the Stainmore road belongs to the movements of Petillius Cerialis, but that the marching-camps could date to the governorship of either Cerialis or Agricola. Four marching- (or campaign-) camps are known in the area – Rey Cross, Crackenthorpe, Kirkby Thore and Plumpton Head;[44] such camps were intended for legions on the march, and consisted of a clear, open, space defended by a rampart-bank, possibly crowned by a palisade (as at Kirkham), and an outer ditch. The space was used for pitching the army's tents. The shapes of these camps are by no means as regular as those of permanent forts: whilst Rey Cross is rectilinear, Plumpton Head forms an irregular trapezoidal shape. The finest of the camps is undeniably Rey Cross, which still has a near-complete rampart-circuit and entrances defended by outer covering mounds (*tutuli*). Recent excavations at Rey Cross have re-vealed 'post-holes' which may have resulted from the use of tent-pegs. Further, the dis-covery of some third-century pottery suggests that the site may have had a use other than simply one that related to the initial conquest of the north-west.

In addition, a line of permanent forts crosses the pass – from Greta Bridge through Bowes, Brough and Kirkby Thore to Broug-ham. Between Bowes and Brough is the much smaller fort of Maiden Castle. Of these, Greta Bridge and Brougham have usually been as-sumed to have been Agricolan foundations, although there is no proof of this: at Kirkby Thore[45] a turf-and-clay rampart inside the later fort may be Agricolan, and a similar defensive arrangement at Bowes was at-tributed to Agricola.[46] Brough-under-Stain-more has seen some excavation,[47] though in the case of this fort, it is the chance finds of

Plate 15. Low Borrow Bridge: The Roman Fort. (*Photograph courtesy of Manunair*)

coins and pottery that point to an Agricolan foundation rather than anything structural revealed by the excavations themselves. Finally, the fortlet at Maiden Castle, which covers approximately half an acre, may well have been more concerned with a signalling and watching role than employed as a garrison fort. Finds have been too few to postulate a chronology: the fortlet was equipped with a stone rampart, and whilst occupation from the Flavian period is not ruled out by the finds, a second-century foundation seems more likely.

Alongside the temporary camps and permanent forts across Stainmore, there are also signal- or watch-towers, three on Stainmore itself, if we include Maiden Castle.[48] Bowes Moor and Roper Castle are closely comparable as oblong earthworks. In recent years, it has been shown that there are other small sites on the western approaches to Stainmore in the form of earthworks made up of a 'platform' with a four-post tower protected by two ditches. Sites of this kind observed and part-tested are Punchbowl Inn, Augill Bridge, Appleby Golf Course and Johnson's Plain.[49] However, a similar earthwork at Augill Castle has been tested, and found not to be of this type: this urges caution in the interpretation of such sites. It has been suggested that the close proximity of these sites one to another was due to the fact that visibility in the area was frequently poor. There is at present no conclusive evidence by which to date these 'western Stainmore' sites, although it is hard to believe that their inception is later than the first century. However, excavation at the rectilinear site at Bowes Moor has produced pottery which is mid-fourth century in date. We thus have to exercise great care in assessing the chronological relationships of the Stainmore sites.

As has already been noted, the Stainmore and north–south roads met at Brougham: the rectangular earthwork of the Roman fort is plainly visible. Whilst there is little dating evidence for the site, it is hardly conceivable that this important road-junction fort does not go back at least to Agricola's period of office.[50]

From Brougham, the main north–south route follows the modern A6 closely. Just north of Penrith lies the fort of Old Penrith: a relatively extensive excavation in 1977–78 produced evidence which suggested that the fort came into operation in the post-Agricolan period, although it must be borne in mind that the excavation was largely concerned with the *vicus* on the south side of the fort, and that it may therefore be premature to infer too much from it about the history of the fort itself.[51] There are at least three other sites in the close vicinity which have been identified from the air. One of these is probably a marching-camp, the other two, though likely military, are of uncertain type. Excavation has suggested that occupation of one of these latter did not begin until the second century.[52]

A number of sites have been located in the vicinity of the road north to Carlisle: at least two marching-camps lie astride the road; also a tilery at Scalesceugh which was producing material from the first to the fourth centuries.[53] Of the presumed forts, Park House is now regarded as a farmstead,[54] whilst both Wreay Hall and Barrock Fell are almost certainly fortlets of considerably later – probably fourth century – date.[55] More recently (1996), another such site – evidently of fourth-century date – has been found close to the newly-discovered fort at Cummersdale. This is in sight of Barrock Fell.

Despite the large amounts of Roman material collected in Carlisle over the years, it is only since the early 1970s that the city has seen a large and near-continuous excavation programme. Roman occupation of many periods has been revealed, although the earliest material currently known comes from two sites separated by more than 400 metres – a civilian building at Blackfriars Street and the spectacular remains of turf-and-timber construction in the Annetwell Street/Abbey Street area. The distance between these two early sites indicates the speed at which Roman Carlisle must have developed in its earliest years.

The excavations of Blackfriars Street[56] have revealed that Blackfriars Street is itself

Plate 16. Brougham: Medieval Castle, sitting on the north-west corner of the Roman fort, which survives as an earthwork of 'playing-card shape'.

on the line of a Roman street of the Flavian period with typical town (*vicus*) building fronting it – long, narrow, 'strip'-buildings, timber-framed, and with their gable-ends facing on to the street. The same type of building can be seen, although in stone-built form, at Vindolanda, and these particular buildings in Carlisle appear to have remained in use into the late fourth and early fifth centuries (see below in chapter 7).

The site in the Annetwell Street/Abbey Street[57] area has seen a considerable amount of excavation since the early 1970s: it is evident that it is military in nature, and five separate phases of fort-construction have been distinguished. The excavations indicated that the southern elements of the fort-defences lay within their area, whilst the bulk of the fort lay to the north under the area subsequently covered by the medieval castle. The development of the fort clearly involved some enlargement, and began with two phases of turf-and-timber construction (between the Flavian and early Antonine periods), two subsequent phases which began *c.* A.D. 165 in which stone buildings were enclosed within turf ramparts, and a final phase in the third century in which the rampart was modified by the addition of a stone wall.

The excavations have been distinguished by the revelation of exceptionally well preserved timbers; dendrochronological tests on these indicate that the inception of the first phase of fort-construction should be placed in the period of Cerialis' governorship (A.D. 71–72), although building-work continued into the Agricolan period. The high standard of preservation of organic material allowed a close study to be undertaken of the south gateway, which has two 'carriageways' of timber, one of which had been so deeply rutted by cart-wheels that it had required replacement. The gateway led to a gravelled roadway inside the fort which had been laid on to a corduroy of logs. The excavations also revealed well preserved sections of turf rampart, also laid on a log corduroy, and climbed by a gravelled service-trackway,

known as an *ascensus*; the *intervallum*-road (interior service road) was located, as well as elements of barracks. There were also sheds of post-and-wattle construction, some of which may have had a connection with leather-tanning. This later feature may suggest that initially at least the site was more akin to a depot than simply a fort, and might therefore prompt a comparison with the Red House site, near Corbridge, at the eastern end of the Stanegate road.

Further significant features have been found to the south of the fort: the excavations in Castle Street revealed signs of industrial activity,[58] and the massive timber platform observed beneath the Museum has yet to be explained. It has sometimes been suggested that the Cathedral overlies significant Roman buildings, but the excavations on the site in 1988 concentrated on later Roman levels. As we shall see (below in chapter 6), the important buildings located in the Lanes excavations serve to emphasise the significance of Carlisle; tile-stamps of all of the British legions have been recovered from the city, and one of the Vindolanda documents refers to the presence there of a *centurio regionarius* – a kind of District Commissioner.[59] The same source refers to *Luguvallium*, making Carlisle one of the few sites in north-west England of which the Roman name is known for certain.

The recently-refined dating for the origin of Roman Carlisle has implications also for the understanding of the Stanegate road. Whilst it is clear that this road was constructed at least as early as Agricola's governorship, it is possible that it should be seen as one of a number of east-west roads for which Cerialis and Agricola were jointly responsible in the early 70s. However, whilst Carlisle and Corbridge were plainly the key-sites on the Stanegate and were both early Flavian in date, the chronology of the other forts and fortlets, apart *possibly* from Nether Denton,[60] is less secure, and will be discussed later in the context of consolidation and frontier-development.

Plate 17. Carlisle: South gateway of the fort (seen from the interior).

Plate 18. Carlisle: Timber rampart-corduroy.

Agricola, then, did not intend to initiate the Stanegate as a conventional frontier, but rather as one of a number of east-west lines (like the Stainmore Pass and the Aire Gap) which served to break up Brigantian territory into segments which could be policed more easily. Agricola's sights were firmly set on further northward advance into Scotland, and presumably a victory over the Caledonians which would allow the whole of Britain to be organised into a province. Emperors, however, had to take a more circumspect view.

Vespasian (A.D. 69–79) had evidently encouraged expansion; the last year of his life coincided with Agricola's third campaign, which took Roman armies up to the line of the Forth and the Clyde. During Titus' short reign (A.D. 79–81), no further advance was made; indeed inscriptions[61] record the removal of some troops from Britain in A.D. 80 for service elsewhere. The preferred solution in Britain had to be balanced against more pressing imperatives in other places. Domitian's accession in A.D. 81 led to a renewed northward drive, though clearly against a background in which some were arguing for the establishment of a frontier on the line of the Forth and Clyde.[62] Agricola (and Tacitus) evidently hoped that doubts were at an end, as is shown by the decision to commence the building of a legionary fortress at Inchtuthil (in Perthshire), implying the permanent posting there of Legion XX *Valeria Victrix*.

Domitian, however, probably viewed the renewed northward advance in more cautious terms; he wanted the Caledonians brought to battle and defeated; this removal of a 'fighting generation' would leave open a number of options – the full incorporation of Scotland into the province, or a breathing-space in which policy could be reviewed. In A.D. 83, Agricola won his battle at the elusive site of *Mons Graupius* (near the Moray Firth), and was almost immediately recalled to Rome. For Tacitus, this was treachery and the prelude to a 'sell-out'; three years later, in A.D. 87, Legion II *Adiutrix* was withdrawn from Britain, and sent to the Danube. The whole of Britain was not to be held, but before we accept Tacitus' negative judgement upon this, we need to understand the character and purpose of the events that followed.

Footnotes

1. *Life of Agricola* 16–17; *Histories* III. 45; *Annals* XII. 40. The latter two are set out in full as Appendix I.
2. *Life of Agricola* 8; Statius *Silvae* v. 2, 31–47.
3. Richmond, 1954; cf. Hartley, 1980.
4. Hanson, 1987, 59–60; Braund, 1984; Hanson and Campbell, 1986; for recent work at Stanwick, see *Britannia* XIII (1982), 348 and XXI (1990), 325.
5. *Life of Agricola* 17.
6. Shotter, 1990, 231; Shotter, 1994.
7. Jones G. D. B., 1968; Jones and Webster, 1968.
8. *Britannia* XI (1980), 365.
9. McPeake, 1978.
10. *Britannia* IX (1978), 436.
11. *Life of Agricola* 25.
12. Evans and Scull, 1990.
13. Birley A. R., 1973.
14. *Life of Agricola* 7–8.
15. Birley A. R., 1973, 188f.
16. For a summary, see *Britannia* XXI (1990), 320.
17. Buxton and Howard-Davis, forthcoming.
18. For a summary of the 1989–90 work at Ribchester, see *Britannia* XXI (1990), 328.
19. *Life of Agricola* 20.
20. Hanson *et al.*, 1979.
21. *RIB* 2434, 1–3
22. Walker, 1989.
23. *Britannia* V (1974), 412f (Troutbeck); *Britannia* XVI (1985), 274 (Brackenrigg).
24. Webster, 1970, 172.
25. Potter, 1979, 151.
26. Graystone, 1992, 13ff.
27. Thompson, 1965, 24ff; Jones M. J., 1975, 142; for further summaries and discussions, see *Britannia* VII (1976), 319ff and VIII (1977), 385ff; also Strickland and Davey, 1978.
28. Jones G. D. B., 1972; Jones M. J., 1975, 170f. For a summary of recent work at the site, see *Britannia* XV (1984), 288.
29. Bruton, 1909; *JRS* LVI (1966), 200.
30. Jones G. D. B., 1974, 23f; *Britannia* VII (1976),

319; XI (1980), 364; XII (1981), 331; XIII (1982), 352; XVII (1986), 385.

31. *Britannia* XV (1984), 286; Jones and Price, 1985; Tindall, 1985.

32. See *Britannia* XIII (1982), 352.

33. For a full discussion of the site, see Walker, 1989; earlier work is brought together in Bruton, 1908 and Start, 1985.

34. Jones M. J., 1975, 166f.

35. Jones and Wild, 1970.

36. Jones M. J., 1975, 149.

37. Jones G. D. B., 1970, 3.

38. Birley E. B., 1946; Hildyard, 1954; Shotter and White, 1995, 36–46.

39. See Jones and Shotter, 1988; Shotter and White, 1990.

40. *RIB* 604.

41. Shotter, 1979.

42. Birley E. B., 1946, 145. The Hadrianic date is attested by the milestone found in the Artle Beck at Caton (*RIB* 2272).

43. Birley E. B., 1947; Hildyard, 1951; For recent discussions, see Shotter and White, 1995, 47–57 and Lambert *et al.*, 1996, 87ff.

44. For Rey Cross and Crackenthorpe, see Richmond and McIntyre, 1934, and *Britannia* XXII (1991), 235f; for Kirkby Thore, see *Britannia*

X (1979), 283; for Plumpton Head, see *Britannia* VI (1975), 232f.

45. For the most recent work, see Gibbons, 1989, particularly p. 108; also Charlesworth, 1964.

46. *JRS* LVII (1968), 179f.

47. Birley E. B., 1958; Jones M. J., 1977.

48. Richmond, 1951.

49. Woolliscroft and Swain, 1991; for the Stainmore sites, see Higham and Jones, 1975.

50. Birley E. B., 1932.

51. Austen, 1991.

52. St. Joseph, 1951; Poulter, 1982.

53. Bellhouse, 1971.

54. Bellhouse, 1954a; Higham and Jones, 1975, 34.

55. Bellhouse, 1953; Collingwood, 1931.

56. McCarthy, 1990.

57. *Britannia* XXI (1990), 320.

58. McCarthy, 1991.

59. Bowman and Thomas, 1983 (Document no. 22); Birley, Birley and Birley, 1993. For a reference on a tablet from Carlisle itself, see *Britannia* XIX (1988), 496.

60. Birley E. B., 1961, 141ff; Jones M. J., 1975, 169.

61. *ILS* 1025 and 9200; see Hanson, 1987, 135.

62. *Life of Agricola* 23 and 25, 2.

4. The Consolidation of the North-West

In territorial terms, much of north-west England had been left untouched in the initial conquest; there is no suggestion that in the years following Agricola's departure there was any serious disturbance to the peace. Clearly, however, the policing network needed to be extended across the area in order to make it effective. But there is no real indication of the chronological development of consolidation, except that it appears to have covered the period from *c.* A.D. 90 to 130.

We have very little help from the literary evidence, with the result that two events dominate – the departure of Agricola and the building of Hadrian's Wall almost forty years later; the period between these events is one of the less well-known episodes in Romano-British history. Yet it contains not only the events that led up to the building of Britain's best-known Roman structure, but also the complete withdrawal from Scotland. For this period, therefore, we are more than ever reliant on scraps of literary information, together with the evidence of inscriptions, and the interpretation of numismatic, ceramic and stratigraphic evidence from the sites themselves.

Tacitus published his biography of Agricola in A.D. 98, two years after the death of the emperor Domitian, about whom the historian was less than enthusiastic; it is clear that he held Domitian as having been maliciously responsible for the fact that Agricola obtained no further post of responsibility after Britain; and there is more than a hint that the emperor may not have been entirely free of having had a hand in Agricola's death in A.D. 93 at the early age of 53. It is hardly likely, therefore, that Tacitus can be regarded as an entirely unbiased source for the events of Domitian's reign.

At the opening of his *Histories*,[1] five Latin words sum up the Flavian achievement in Britain, as Tacitus saw it: 'Britain was totally conquered, and immediately allowed to slip'. In a sense, we can confirm Tacitus' judgement by noting the situation at Agricola's departure, where the Caledonians had been defeated at *Mons Graupius* in north-east Scotland,[2] and where there seemed no further enemy left – except the terrain: with it we may compare the extremely cryptic reference by Spartianus, the biographer of Hadrian,[3] to the fact that at the time of Trajan's death in the east in A.D. 117, 'the Britons could not be kept under Roman control'. Between these two dates we know that one of Agricola's successors in Britain, Sallustius Lucullus, was executed allegedly for having named a new type of lance after himself:[4] since this happened in A.D. 89 it is likely that it was not unconnected with a serious rebellion on the Rhine, instigated by one Antonius Saturninus. Further, the poet Juvenal in a satire about Domitian's court[5] mentions hopes of capturing Arviragus of the Britons – obviously a name of some contemporary significance to find a place in a work intended for a Roman audience. He also refers in another satire[6] to soldiers 'blooding' themselves in battle with the Brigantes – which must presumably have a 'dramatic date' of *c.* A.D. 100. That little love was lost between members of the Roman army and local Britons seems clear from the Vindolanda-document which talks of *Britunculi* ('nasty little Brits').[7]

The only other piece of documentary evidence consists of a coin of Hadrian, bearing the legend BRITANNIA[8] – distinct from the BRITANNIA coin issued a little later in the reign to commemorate Hadrian's journey to Britain. The coin was issued in A.D. 119 – that is, during the governorship of Quintus Pompeius Falco, – and must surely refer to victories which were the result of Hadrian's initial response to the problems alluded to by Spartianus. The recent discovery (1996) at Vindolanda of an inscription (dated to A.D.

119) referring to the death in war of a centurion appears to provide further evidence of these late Trajanic and early Hadrianic difficulties.

When Agricola was replaced in A.D. 83, the initial imperative was the clarification of the arrangements in the far north – whether the aim of total conquest was to be pursued or whether a territorial compromise would be necessary. Although the building work on Agricola's northern Scottish sites was evidently continued under his successor,[9] by A.D. 87 a decision appears to have been reached to abandon this work, including that on the legionary fortress at Inchtuthil. It has always been assumed that the evacuation of Scotland was managed in two phases: a withdrawal to a frontier between the Forth and the Clyde in c. A.D. 87, followed a decade or so later by a withdrawal from the Scottish lowlands to the Stanegate Road, which linked the Tyne and the Solway. Recent studies, however,[10] have demonstrated that this 'traditional' hypothesis requires reconsideration. The attraction of an 'intermediate frontier' on the Forth/Clyde line had always been that it is mentioned by Tacitus[11] in the context of Agricola's campaigns, and was indeed fortified by him during his fourth season in A.D. 80.[12]

As suggested above (in chapter 3), the victory of *Mons Graupius* laid the ground for two obvious options – total conquest or a strategic withdrawal to a point at which consolidation was regarded as desirable and feasible; a withdrawal *on Roman terms* would not be seen as a 'sell-out'. The evidence of coin-loss[13] on Roman sites in Scotland demonstrates the strong likelihood that a general evacuation was organised in c. A.D. 87; only the major sites of Newstead and Dalswinton appear to have been left – perhaps as outliers of a new frontier-system. This was, of course, the same year that saw the transfer of Legion II *Adiutrix*, presumably with some auxiliaries, to the Danube-region.

There is no sign that this represented a rushed decision; indeed, the decision had probably been taken already at the time of

Plate 19. Troutbeck: Entrance of marching-camp.

Plate 20. Vindolanda: Fort and *vicus*. (*Photograph courtesy of Manunair*)

Agricola's recall. During the intervening period work was probably put in train for the development of the Stanegate-frontier – in particular, the construction of a series of large forts which would be required to receive the considerable number of troops returning from Scotland. Thus, it seems likely that the forts of the Stanegate were built not as a response to withdrawal, but in preparation for it. If the decision was taken with this degree of deliberation, then we might begin to comprehend – though not accept – Tacitus' clear feelings of a betrayal of Agricola's work.

The main series of forts, each of seven to eight acres – Corbridge, Newbrough, Vindolanda, Carvoran, Nether Denton, Brampton and Carlisle – was in place by the late 80s; it is possible that the newly-discovered fort at Cummersdale also fitted into this context. The stratigraphic complexity of sites, such as Corbridge and Vindolanda, indicates that considerable modifications must have been undertaken in the decades before the decision to build Hadrian's Wall. A major revision involved the reduction in size of the principal

forts by approximately fifty percent, and the introduction of intermediate structures, such as fortlets (for example, Haltwistle, Throp and Boothby) and watchtowers (for example, Pike Hill). Such arrangements brought the Stanegate more obviously into line with frontiers in other parts of the empire.[14]

Extensions to the Stanegate were built at both ends, though the precise dating of these is not easy to determine. In the east, the Stanegate was continued to a fort at Whickham (Washing Well) and perhaps to the Tyne-estuary and a new fort at South Shields. Far greater complexity, however, has been detected west of Carlisle;[15] linear features, with intermediate structures, run from Carlisle to a fort (and presumably a significant anchorage) at Kirkbride. It has been suggested[16] that this may have been a depot referred to in a Vindolanda-document as *Briga*. It appears[17] that a ditch and palisade ran westwards across Solway with intermediate watchtowers; it occupied the higher ground to the rear of the mosses rather than the foreshore. The linear features have been observed at a number of places, including Farnhill and Finglandrigg, and it has been demonstrated that they were secondary to four-posted watchtowers which sat in an ovoid ditched enclosure. Such watchtowers have been tested at Easton and Farnhill, and one of them found beneath the rampart-material of a large fort (of eight acres) at Burgh-by-Sands.[18] In its turn, this large fort, as with the main Stanegate-series, had been subsequently reduced in size by a half.

The purposes of such arrangements, which again recall those in place on the Rhine, might be to afford protected communications from the supposed depot at Kirkbride to Carlisle, which, from the presence there of a *centurio regionarius* ('District Commissioner'), might be seen as the western headquarters of the Stanegate-system. However, it seems hard to divorce these structures from a role of protecting the important land of Carvetian farmers from harrassment from across the Solway. Little dating-evidence has been recovered, but it might be tempting to see the large and reduced forts at Burgh-by-Sands as contemporary with the similar sequence on the Stanegate, which would have the effect of leaving the linear features as earlier (perhaps Agricolan). It is worth bearing in mind that the southern flank of the Solway Plain seems to have enjoyed at an early stage a protection from the south by means of a line from Carlisle to the coast through the large fort at Blennerhasset; it is further likely that development at Cummersdale should be related to this also. Further complexity is suggested by the discovery of a similar watchtower on Gamelsby Ridge and at Crooklands (between

Plate 21. Nether Denton: Forts. (*Photograph courtesy of Manunair*)

Plate 22. Burgh-by-Sands: Stanegate-forts; ramparts arrowed. (*Photograph courtesy of Manunair*)

Plate 23.
Burgh-by-Sands:
Watchtower
beneath the
Trajanic fort-
rampart.
(*Photograph
courtesy of
G. D. B. Jones*)

33

Plate 24. Finglandrigg: Section of running-ditch, which was part of the Solway-fortifications.

left untouched (figure 4). It is largely through critical studies of the pottery and coin-loss evidence that we have come to recognise the sites that are post-Agricolan in date. The chief forts that pierce and surround the Lake District, in addition to those Agricolan and probable Agricolan sites on the Lune and the Eden, are Old Carlisle, Papcastle, Caermote, Old Penrith, Troutbeck, Ambleside, Hardknott, Ravenglass and Watercrook: as well as these there are the coastal forts of Beckfoot, Maryport, Burrow Walls and Moresby, which will be discussed more fully in the next chapter.

Few of these have seen large-scale work; in the north, a road ran from Carlisle in a south-westerly direction through Old Carlisle (Red Dial), Caermote and Papcastle to the coast at Maryport. Old Carlisle,[19] a fort with an extensive and evidently well-preserved *vicus*, is virtually untouched by excavation, and so no chronology can be proposed for the site. Papcastle[20] has seen a large excavation in the mid-1980s on an important *vicus*-building, which has provided evidence of

Kirkbride and Beckfoot). Clearly, there is much yet to be understood about these arrangements, though they are in no circumstances suggestive of a negative 'sell-out'.

Thus one, perhaps the major, element of the post-Agricolan consolidation was the provision of a visible frontier to the north of the province. As we have already seen, the Lake District appears to have been the major part of north-west England which Agricola had

Plate 25. Watercrook: Roman Fort, situated in a 'bow' of the river Kent.

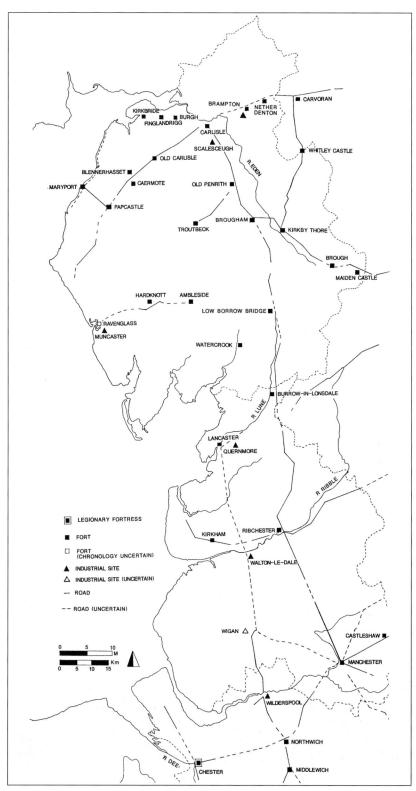

Figure 4.
Pre-Hadrianic
sites in North-
West England.

possible military connections with eastern Europe. Earlier work revealed evidence of timber structures and artefactual material which, though not decisive, do not rule out a late Flavian origin.[21] The fact that the fort is larger than many may single it out as having special responsibilities in the north Lakes. At Caermote,[22] two turf-and-timber forts have been found, one inside the other. The larger is the earlier fort, and a Trajanic date for the larger, and a Hadrianic date for the smaller, would not be inconsistent with the evidence. The dating evidence would not appear to support the Agricolan foundation which has been argued on grounds of gateway-style.

On the eastern side of the Lakes, recent excavation at Old Penrith has argued for a date not earlier than the late Flavian period,[23] although it should be remembered that chronological coincidence between fort and *vicus* occupation should not necessarily be assumed. Brougham fort has produced no evidence, though burials in the cemetery were dated to the second and third centuries A.D.[24] At Low Borrow Bridge, as we have seen, there is some suggestion of an enlargement of the fort in the form of a pebbly-clay rampart which may have been associated with a stone wall: however, even if the interpretation is correct, dating remains hazardous, although a second-century date for the 'larger' fort cannot be ruled out.[25] Between Penrith and Keswick, in the vicinity of the known marching-camp at Troutbeck, lies a newly-recognised fort site. Although not firmly dated, this fort had a rampart of clay blocks, and would fit the policing network. At some later date this fort was reduced in size.[26]

Relatively large-scale excavations were carried out at Ambleside (Waterhead) earlier in the century, and revealed a slightly irregular rectangular fort defended by clay ramparts. Outside there were two and, in places, three ditches. The central range of buildings was uncovered, though relating to a later stone-

Plate 26. Ambleside (Waterhead): The Granaries of the Roman fort.

built phase of the fort. On the basis of the pottery the foundation of the fort has been assigned to the late Flavian period.[27] It is, however, worth noting that during site clearance in 1982 approximately half a mile to the north of the fort, features were observed which would not be inconsistent with a defensive system, though associated pottery was largely second-century in date.

The position of the Ambleside fort at the head of Lake Windermere emphasises its peculiar advantage in that men and materials could be carried to the fort by ship independently of the road-system. This in its turn serves to emphasise the continuing elusiveness of Roman sites in southern Cumbria which would have been linked to Ambleside by the lake. It is worth noting that in the 1970s, divers at the north end of Lake Windermere recognised large worked and perforated stones which would not be inconsistent with jetty-structures.[28]

Presumably as part of the policing arrangements for the Lake District, a road was eventually driven through from Ambleside to the coast at Ravenglass. Although we now know that the latter site is of Hadrianic date, the intermediate fort at Hardknott is now regarded as having a Trajanic foundation.[29] This almost square fort is superbly sited with excellent visibility down Eskdale to the sea. The fort is stone-built, although it is assumed that a rampart-bank was originally provided and it had two ditches where necessary: on parts of the site, however, natural features obviated the need to cut ditches. Excavation of interior features revealed two phases of barrack block – of timber and stone.

Ravenglass[30] will be discussed more fully in its coastal context in the next chapter, but for the present purpose it is sufficient to say that the most recent excavations suggest that a mid-Hadrianic fort was preceded by an early Hadrianic fortlet on a different alignment. The dating of the other coastal forts is hazardous: Maryport, of which a stone wall and rampart have been recovered, appears on coin and pottery evidence to be a late Flavian

or, more likely, Trajanic foundation. However, in view of the evident complexity of arrangements in Solway (discussed above), it may be that an earlier fort awaits discovery nearby – or even beneath the known fort.[31] Of Moresby, Burrow Walls and Beckfoot, little is known, apart from the Hadrianic building-inscription from Moresby,[32] which has prompted the plausible suggestion[33] that on the coastal system some at least of the forts may have represented a later addition – as, of course, they did on Hadrian's Wall itself.

Further south, recent work at Watercrook,[34] although largely confined to the *vicus*, has suggested that the first phase, recognised in a clay-and-turf rampart, should not be placed earlier than late Flavian times. On the east angle, the outer defences consisted of three ditches: between the first and second was a palisade and a stone bank. The fort, which is nearly square, was protected on three sides by a bow of the River Kent, prompting the suggestion that it, rather than Hardknott, may be MEDIBOGDO of the *Ravenna Cosmography* – the name meaning 'fort in the middle of a bow' which closely describes Watercrook's disposition.

Thus consolidation work in the Lake District had the effect of driving east-west policing lines from the main north–south route in the direction of the coast. Field work also suggests the linking of some of these sites by north–south roads, which would thus have the effect of imposing an informal 'grid' on the area. One unanswered question concerns the southern fringes of the Lakes: no sites have been recovered, although the volume of finds in the Cartmel and Barrow areas suggests the possible existence of sites in Furness.[35] It is similarly possible that further sites await discovery on the coastline of western Cumbria – for example, between Moresby and Ravenglass, and between Ravenglass and Barrow. In the former case it is worth noting the substantial amount of material to have come from the Beckermet area.[36]

The picture across Stainmore[37] in the con-

Plate 27. Hardknott: Roman fort.

Plate 28. Hardknott: Parade-ground (to the east of the fort).

solidation period is unclear. At Greta Bridge, occupation from late Flavian times is assumed on the basis of finds, whilst at Bowes the elaborate Flavian (Agricolan) rampart was modified, though at a date not certainly proved. The fort at Brough, as noted above, has produced no clear evidence of its structural sequence, though its long-term importance is attested by the large collection of lead sealings of various army units found there.

Kirkby Thore certainly had a second phase turf-and-clay rampart, though its date is uncertain.

Further south, other Pennine routes received attention: Castleshaw, as we have seen, was reduced in size – the Agricolan fort of three acres being replaced by one of 0.6 acres built inside the earlier fort: whilst the second fort was undoubtedly of the second century, the exact date of its construction is unclear.[38] The changes of size, noted here and elsewhere in the north-west, must surely indicate considerable garrison modifications over the years.

Whilst consolidation in Cumbria basically meant the laying out of a new fort-system, the military framework of Lancashire and Cheshire already existed. At Burrow-in-Lonsdale it appears that the presumed Agricolan turf-and-timber fort was modified and realigned, but at what date cannot be determined.[39] It is not unreasonable, however, to assume that a fair life-span for a turf-and-timber fort might have been twenty to twenty-five years before major modification and repair were required. In this case, provided that there was not a break in occupation at Burrow, a Trajanic date for the modifications would seem reasonable.

At the mouth of the Lune, Lancaster too underwent modification; in this case, a Trajanic building inscription[40] gives a clear indication and is presumably to be associated with the clay rampart and stone wall resting on a bevelled plinth course observed to the north of the old Vicarage. As noted above, this line of defence represented an enlargement of the earliest fort, and possibly its re-orientation through 90 degrees so that the main gate moved from the east to the north. Similarly, traces of the eastern gateway of a stone fort were excavated close to the junction of Church Street and China Street.

The Ribble forts also underwent modification. The addition of a stone wall to the first-phase rampart at Kirkham could conceivably have been Trajanic.[41] At Ribchester the evident complication of the site makes interpretation far more difficult. It is clear that the fort went through a number of modifications whilst retaining turf-and-timber construction. These modifications may have included a re-alignment through 90 degrees, which may also have involved a change in size and garrison. Evidence does exist to show that the Asturian cavalry, apparently based at Ribchester in the late first and early second centuries, was moved to Hadrian's Wall. It was to this unit that the famous parade-helmet belonged.[42]

Further, the coin-series from Ribchester is not inconsistent with a break in occupation at some time in the Hadrianic period. Later in the second century A.D., part of the consignment of Danubian Sarmatians, sent to Britain by Marcus Aurelius, was deployed at Ribchester. This may indicate further structural modifications, which apparently included the addition to the original turf rampart of a stone fort-wall which has been recovered in some, but not all, of the excavations. The stone phase evidently therefore belongs to the re-aligned fort, and it is assumed that the stone granaries which are visible at the rear of the Museum were part of this later fort-phase. The stone-building may be as late as Severan − (that is, early third century) − in date.[43] A further importance of Ribchester is deduced from the form of the name of the site which is given in the Ravenna Cosmography as BRESNETENACI VETERANORUM. The name implies a settlement of especial significance outside the fort, the body of which was made up of discharged soldiers. There has been much speculation regarding the purpose and effect of these, including the possibility that land was allocated to them in the Fylde (see below in chapter 6). Although no explicit indication of their presence has emerged from the archaeological record, it is possible that bank-and-ditch features which have been observed in two locations at a distance from the fort could be part of the defences provided for a settlement which had a quasi-military purpose.

At Manchester, recent excavations[44] have demonstrated two turf-and-timber phases, the later of the two representing an enlargement of the fort from approximately four to five acres, apparently early in the second century. The mid-second century − possibly c. A.D. 165 − saw the addition of a stone wall to the later rampart. The same structural sequence has been observed both in the western defences and in the area of the north gateway. Further south at Northwich,[45] two phases of fort were recognised − an Agricolan phase which lasted until early in the second century, which was followed by the building of a wall to the front of the rampart. The commencement date of phase II was not precisely placed, but is probably Antonine. The site's later industrial activity will be discussed below (in chapter 6).

Excavations of the legionary fortress at Chester[46] have shown that it, too, shared in the work of consolidation: as noted above, the original fortification of Chester probably goes back to late-Neronian times, but the Abbey Green excavations showed that the Flavian fortress itself underwent a number of modifications before the Trajanic rebuilding in stone, which is recorded on an inscription.[47]

Thus it can be seen that in Lancashire and Cheshire the consolidation period represented a chronologically fairly uniform process of rebuilding and often enlarging Agricola's forts early in the Trajanic period; this fact incidentally can be regarded as confirmation of Tacitus' observation about Agricola's good eye for fort placement.[48]

It is stated by Tacitus that the results of Agricola's campaigns in their effects on the native population were dramatic – in terms of the abandonment of hostility and the acceptance of garrisons. It seems to suggest a very similar situation to that described by Dio Cassius as having obtained in Germany in the Augustan period[49] – that 'the barbarians were adapting themselves to Roman ways, were becoming accustomed to hold markets, and were meeting in peaceful assemblages ... and were becoming different without knowing it.' This certainly implies a rapid establishment of peace: in a sense, the growth outside the forts of civilian settlements (*vici*), which were presumably in the main undefended, tends to

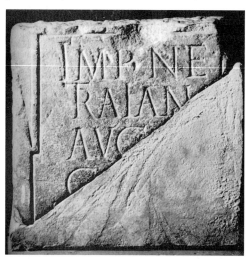

Plate 29. Lancaster: Trajanic building-inscription. The inscription reads: 'To the Emperor, Nerva Trajan Caesar Augustus Germanicus Dacicus, Consul ... saluted as *Imperator*'. (*Lancaster City Museum and Art Gallery*)

confirm this. It can be shown that the majority of the forts saw *vici* established very soon after their own initial foundation, as local people and those from further afield positioned themselves to take advantage of the markets provided by the soldiers *and*, of course, by each other.

However, a further indication of the positive nature of the post-Agricolan arrangements is provided by the evidence which survives of the development of the infrastructure necessary for the supply of the garrisons. It seems likely that at first much of the army's portable requirements were supplied by contracts with travelling salesmen and overseas suppliers. Early on, however, building-materials and everyday pottery-requirements were transferred, at least in part, to the initiative and organisation of individual units. As we have seen, a manufacturing-facility was provided at Scalesceugh for the supply of Carlisle: similar sites are known to have existed at Quernmore (for Lancaster) and Brampton.[50]

In the late first century, however, the *vici* appear to have provided space dedicated to manufacturing. At Manchester,[51] for example, an area was given over to metal-working, and similar arrangements probably obtained elsewhere; such arrangements presuppose the exploitation of local raw materials, in much the same way, as is shown by Vindolanda-documents, as greater organisation was introduced into the exploitation of local agricultural resources.

The smaller, localised, facilities were, from the late years of the first century A.D., supplemented by rather larger undertakings, which will be discussed more fully in chapter 6. Salt-extraction and processing is attested at a number of sites in Cheshire, principally Northwich, Middlewich and Nantwich,[52] whilst larger multi-purposed, manufacturing centres developed at Holt, Heronbridge, Wilderspool, and possibly Wigan also.[53] Whilst that at Holt may have been directly a military facility, producing pottery and building-materials, the others were probably *organised* by the army, although the workers were evidently of local origin. It would not be in-appropriate, particularly in the case of Wil-derspool, to see this as a site concerned with a wide range of products, organised by the Roman army by encouraging local manufac-turers and traders into an environment which gave them better access to their markets. That manufacturers were of local origin is strongly suggested by the presence of so-called 'trade-mark' stamps on pottery, which probably represent the blundered attempts of illiterate people to copy potters' marks[54] – parallel, in fact to the blundered legends on copied radi-ate-coins of the late third century.

This improved organisation probably lay behind the re-development of Walton-le-Dale,[55] on the southern side of the river Ribble. As we have seen, there are indications that it started as a fort until the earliest years of the Flavian period. After a break of occu-pation which lasted until the end of the first century, a new phase of activity is apparent in the form of long, rectangular, shed-like buildings, constructed of timber. The regu-larity of these is persuasive of a military origin and purpose, though no clear traces that re-vealed that purpose emerged during the ex-cavation of the site. It is perhaps best to suggest that the buildings were for the storage presumably of military supplies prior to their deployment elsewhere in the north-west. The site retained this character into the early third century A.D., after which signs of occupation at Walton-le-Dale are far more ephemeral.

However, whilst the work of Agricola and his successors certainly represents overall a positive achievement, and whilst, as we have seen, there is evidence which implies settled conditions, it is nonetheless true that the mili-tary could not afford to relax: a tight 'polic-ing' network had been constructed, although this could of course break down, particularly in areas where movement was difficult. As we have seen, the evidence of field work and excavation, combined with the comment of Spartianus, shows that conditions in the north of the region in the early second century had become tense and dangerous – perhaps because of further troop withdrawals in con-nection with Trajan's Dacian and Parthian wars. It is certainly evident that Hadrian's reappraisal in A.D. 117 showed him that the Trajanic level of military momentum was neither desirable nor practicable. Further, there is some evidence from early imperial coin-hoards in Lancashire[56] that conditions had become less settled in the south of the region also.

It is clear that Hadrian 'stopped the rot' – initially by intervention through his governor, Pompeius Falco. The longer-term and more radical solution, which may in fact be regarded as the culmination of consolidation, was the building of a new frontier – this time not a road, but a continuous barrier – Hadrian's Wall.

Footnotes

1. *Histories* I. 2.
2. For recent discussions of the possible site of this battle, see Hanson, 1987, 127ff and Max-well, 1990.
3. *Scriptores Historiae Augustae (SHA), Life of Hadrian* 5,2.
4. Suetonius, *Life of Domitian* 10.
5. *Satires* IV. 127.
6. *Satires* XIV. 196.
7. See Birley, Birley and Birley, 1993, 37.
8. Hill, 1970, 154ff; (*RIC* II (Hadrian), 577).
9. Hanson, 1987, 53.
10. Jones G. D. B., 1990.
11. *Life of Agricola* 23 and 25, 2.
12. *Life of Agricola* 23; Shotter, 1996, 34f.
13. Hobley, 1989.
14. Breeze and Dobson, 1976, 20ff; Breeze, 1982, 60ff.
15. Jones G. D. B., 1982.
16. Birley, Birley and Birley, 1993, 39.
17. Jones G. D. B., 1994/5.
18. *Britannia* X (1979), 281–2.
19. Birley E. B., 1951.
20. *Britannia* XVI (1985), 276.

21. Birley E. B., 1963; Charlesworth, 1965.
22. Bellhouse, 1960a; Jones M. J., 1975, 135.
23. Austen, 1991.
24. *JRS* LVII (1967), 177; *JRS* LVIII (1968), 179.
25. Jones M. J., 1975, 164; Lambert *et al.*, 1996, 87ff.
26. Jones M. J., 1975, 180; Allan, 1994, 8ff.
27. Hartley, 1966, 12; for work to the north of the fort, see Leech, 1993; for more recent work, see *Britannia* XXI (1990), 320 and Mann and Dunwell, 1995.
28. Shotter, 1995.
29. Hartley, 1966, 12; *JRS* LV (1965), 203; Jones M. J., 1975, 154f.
30. Potter, 1979, 48f.
31. Jarrett, 1976.
32. *RIB* 801; this inscription is dated to post – A.D. 128.
33. Potter, 1979, 359.
34. For the excavations of 1974–5 and a discussion of results, see Potter, 1979.
35. Shotter, 1995.
36. Shotter, 1980, 163.
37. Greta Bridge (Jones M. J., 1975, 154); Bowes (Jones M. J., 1975, 130f); Brough-under-Stainmore (Richmond, 1936; Jones M. J., 1977); Kirkby Thore (Jones M. J., 1975, 158; Gibbons, 1989).
38. Walker, 1989.
39. Jones M. J., 1975, 134; Shotter and White, 1995, 36ff.
40. *RIB* 604; Shotter and White, 1990.
41. Jones M. J., 1975, 159; Buxton and Howard-Davis, forthcoming.
42. Edwards, 1992.
43. For a summary of the most recent work at Ribchester, see *Britannia* XXI (1990), 328 and Buxton, 1996, 11–18. Earlier work has been published in Edwards and Webster, 1985–1988.
44. *Britannia* XI (1980), 364; XIII (1982), 353; XVII (1986), 385.
45. *Britannia* XV (1984), 288.
46. Thompson, 1965, 24ff; Strickland and Davey, 1978.
47. *RIB* 464; *Britannia* IX (1978), 429f.
48. *Life of Agricola* 22.
49. Dio Cassius, *History of Rome* LVI. 18, 2.
50. Quernmore, see Leather and Webster, 1988, 85ff; Brampton, see Hogg, 1965. Cf. Muncaster (Bellhouse, 1960b) and Scalesceugh (*Britannia* II (1971), 251).
51. Jones G. D. B., 1974.
52. Thompson, 1965, 88ff.
53. For Heronbridge, see Thompson, 1965, 60ff; for Holt, see Grimes, 1930 and Thompson, 1965, 53ff; for Wilderspool, see Hinchliffe and Williams, 1992 and Strickland, 1995; for Wigan, see Jones and Price, 1985 and Tindall, 1985.
54. Hartley and Webster, 1973, 92–95.
55. See *Britannia* XIII (1982), 352.
56. Shotter, 1978b; Shotter, 1990, 129ff.

5. *The Northern Frontier*

The events in the northern frontier area in the first two decades of the second century are, as we have seen, riddled with interpretative problems. The only certain element is that there was disturbance – possibly throughout the whole of the north-west. It seems that this trouble had first to be dealt with, and then a more lasting answer found to it. By inference we can assume that Hadrian's view was that, alone, the Stanegate system was inadequate.

Hadrian himself came to Britain in A.D. 121 or 122 – evidently almost the first of his long series of imperial visits.[1] Apart from the introduction of a new policy, two further, presumably related, changes may be discerned: the governor, Quintus Pompeius Falco, was replaced by Aulus Platorius Nepos (A.D. 122–125), and Legion IX *Hispana* at York was replaced by Legion VI *Victrix*, previously garrisoned at Vetera (Xanten) on the Rhine. Nepos' earlier career had given him service as governor of Lower Germany, whilst the legion must have had extensive experience of frontier works on the Rhine (*Limes Germanicus*), and it has been suggested[2] that the legion may have come straight from the Rhine to the Tyne. Although Legion IX *Hispana* had not over the years had a happy time in Britain and may well have suffered in the recent disturbances, the well-known story of its disappearance is romantic fiction. That the new policy was Hadrian's own is attested by his biographer, Spartianus: 'He made for Britain, where he set right many things and – the first to do so – drew a wall along a length of eighty miles to separate barbarians and Romans'.

A detailed discussion of Hadrian's Wall is beyond the scope of the present work;[3] comment will thus be restricted to more general observations. It is evident that in the first instance Hadrian's Wall was seen as a unity with the Stanegate, since although small patrols (perhaps approximately twenty men each) were housed in the milecastles, the main bodies of troops at first remained in the Stanegate forts. Whilst the Stanegate ran through the valleys of the Tyne, Irthing and Eden rivers, the Wall occupied the northern crests of those valleys. In all, then, this will have had the effect of retaining the policing potential of the traditional *limes* and added to it the ability both to see and deal with threats from the north. It was thus in effect a 'barrier-*limes*' that cut through northern Brigantian territory, controlling traffic and the inter-connection of groups whose combination we must assume to have been considered hazardous. The Wall, with the enormous strategic advantage it gained from such natural features as the Great Whin Sill, will have greatly enhanced the policing potential of the Stanegate since it will have relieved pressure from the northern flank of that line.

The original plan seems to have included the Wall itself, a ditch to the north (not cut where natural features made it unnecessary), and milecastles every Roman mile, between each pair of which were two square turrets. With installations so closely-spaced, lateral communications along the wall were clearly at a premium. The construction-work evidently began in the east, as is shown by an inscription, possibly from Jarrow,[4] and was designed to run from Newcastle. Eventually, however, it was extended to an eastern terminus at Wallsend. The Wall ran to Bowness-on-Solway in the west; its eastern two-thirds (as far as the Irthing Gap) were built of stone, whilst the western third was of turf, with installations (except the watchtowers) of turf-and-timber construction. A fragmentary wooden inscription from Milecastle 50 places this work in Nepos' governorship.

The reason for the change in building-materials on the western sector has often been discussed – with various solutions proposed.

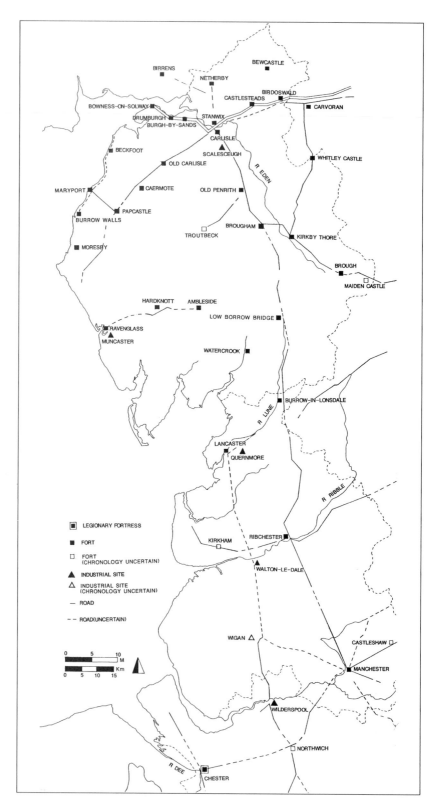

Figure 5.
Sites in North-
West England
occupied at the
death of Had-
rian (A.D. 138)

44

Plate 30. Cawfields: Hadrian's Wall, milecastle and *vallum*. (*Photograph courtesy of Manunair*)

Possibly it was the paucity of good building-stone or limestone for mortar, at least close enough at hand to make quarrying a worth-while and/or safe undertaking. This might be of relevance if, as many have supposed, the chief problems with local tribesmen lay in the west. We should, however, remember that for most of the occupation of the north to that time, turf and timber had been regarded as perfectly adequate materials: we should not therefore necessarily assume that in the Roman mind the materials of the western sector were markedly inferior in capability to the stone of the east. The chief problem would be a longer-term one – namely, that the turf-and-timber structures would presum-ably require major renovation before the stonework.

However, a more radical possibility sug-gests itself; when the Antonine Wall was built in Scotland in the mid-second century A.D., there are indications that the initial approach differed from the plan finally adopted.[5] It appears that local commanders expected that,

like Hadrian's Wall, the Antonine Wall would be constructed of stone; the fort at Balmuildy was itself built of stone and equipped at its northern corners with project-ing stone wings, as if it was expected that the fort would be joined by a stone wall. It is possible that events progressed in a similar fashion on Hadrian's Wall. As we have seen, we have no detailed information of the nature or extent of the difficulties which were pla-guing the north in the last years of Trajan's reign. If the heart of the troubles lay in the north-west, then local commanders *may*, on a general instruction, have commenced build-ing-work in the west, using materials which they regarded as normal. Hadrian's pref-erence for stone – an unusual choice for such a structure – probably reflects his enthusiasm for architecture and his awareness of the pol-itical impact of buildings. It is worth bearing in mind that recent excavations at Birdoswald have revealed a section of extraordinarily fine masonry at the foot of the southern guardchamber of the west gate: it is not

Plate 31. Hadrian's Wall: Housesteads fort.

inconceivable that this was the remnant of an earlier structure, such as a trophy erected to commemorate the victory of Pompeius Falco which had restored the equilibrium and which was commemorated by Hadrian on his coinage.[6]

Platorius Nepos was replaced as governor in A.D. 125 or 126; at about this time the decision was evidently made to bring the main bodies of troops on to the wall itself and to build forts for them there. Recent excavation at Bowness-on-Solway[7] has suggested that the process may not have been chronologically uniform over the entire wall, and certainly Carrawburgh, by its relationship with the *vallum*, can be shown to have been an 'after-thought' (*c*. A.D. 133). In effect, therefore, the Stanegate forts of Chesterholm (Vindolanda), Nether Denton and Brampton were advanced to Housesteads, Great Chesters, Birdoswald and Castlesteads, whilst at Carvoran the Wall and the Stanegate were close enough for the fort to be retained. At Carlisle, a new fort was built at Stanwix, although recent excavation suggests that this did not mean the loss of a garrison at Carlisle itself. On the western Stanegate, the sites of Burgh I, Finglandrigg, and Kirkbride were 'advanced' respectively to Burgh II, Drumburgh and Bowness-on-Solway. The relationship between the 'fort phase' and the 'pre-fort phase' had been convincingly demonstrated by the discovery that some of the forts overlie already existing Wall-installations – for example, at Housesteads.[8] We should also note that in the western sector the turf wall was equipped with turf-and-timber forts, although the watchtowers (turrets) were built of stone throughout. Recent excavations have demonstrated that, contrary to previous expectations, a turf-and-timber phase preceded the stone fort at Birdoswald.[9]

To the south of the forts, and evidently part of the same plan, ran the *vallum*, the name used for the feature since Bede's time. This consisted of a flat-bottomed ditch, some

Plate 32. Hadrian's Wall: Birdoswald fort.

Plate 33. Birdoswald: The west gate, showing the fine quality of the masonry of the southern guard-chamber.

Plate 34. Birdoswald: The south granary.

eight feet deep, with steep sides. When kept clean, it would have been extremely hard for an intruder to extricate himself from it: north and south of the *vallum*-ditch were cleared areas (or berms), bounded by continuous mounds of earth made up of the upcast from the ditch and carefully revetted with turf. The feature, which runs the whole length of the wall on its southern side (except for the eastern extension to Wallsend) was 120 feet wide overall. Its purpose has been much discussed, but it would appear to have demarcated a military zone on the southern side of the wall, and possibly acted as a 'man-trap' – thus either keeping out unauthorised people or getting them into a position where they would not easily be able to get across to the north of the wall, and perhaps trap them until they were rounded up by patrols. An alternative explanation of its purpose is that the *vallum*-ditch provided a concealed communications-route, perhaps for covert deployment of troops.

The *vallum* may perhaps give us a clue as to why the 'fort-phase' of the wall was undertaken: a military zone which consisted of the wall, the Stanegate and intervening territory was perhaps too wide in most areas for convenience or efficiency as well as security. For example, the distance between Kirkbride and its 'wall-equivalent', Bowness-on-Solway, is four miles. In this connection, it is worth noting that even in a communications role the Stanegate was superseded by the military way which ran in the Wall/*vallum* corridor.

The whole system was in place probably by the mid-130s. However, the replacement of turf-and-timber by stone structures is hard to place chronologically. It has been suggested that this work may have been done late in Hadrian's reign,[10] or possibly after the evacu-ation of the Antonine Wall in the 160s. In recent years, however, excavation at Bowness-on-Solway failed to provide a firm date for the inception of the stone phase, whilst those at Birdoswald have suggested that at that fort the work could be as late as the Severan period.[11] It might therefore be safest to assume that this particular type of modification did not belong to a single plan, but was carried out over a period. Indeed, the record of building-inscriptions from Hadrian's Wall suggests that there was a near-continuous building-programme from the 160s into the early years of the third century.[12]

Three outpost forts were provided in the west to the north of the Wall – at Birrens, Netherby and Bewcastle. It is argued[13] that these were not 'early-warning' forts, but placed to protect that part of Brigantian territory which was cut off by the Wall – an argument which receives some force from the discovery of the Romanised *Brigantia*-relief at Birrens. It is further argued that since these forts are tied to Hadrian's Wall by a road, which runs to Milecastle 50 rather than to

Plate 35. Bewcastle: The western ramparts of the polygonal fort.

Birdoswald, they were part of the original plan, though not necessarily actually built until the mid-Hadrianic period. Notable amongst these is Bewcastle, which abandons the normal rectangular shape in favour of an irregular polygon encompassing a hill-top: this was presumably intended to give it good visibility in what might be expected to be troubled terrain.[14]

It should be borne in mind that the construction of the Wall and its installations will have caused considerable disruption in a populated area – not just the major disruption of separating kinsmen from each other, but, on a more individual level, requiring the ejection of families from the farms that represented their livelihoods.[15]

The wall-forts were all of a size to accommodate complete units.[16] The average acreage is approximately five, with the two largest at Bowness-on-Solway and Stanwix (9.32). Despite some confusions over the names of Hadrian's Wall forts,[17] there seems no doubt that Stanwix housed the milliary *Ala Petriana*, and was the Wall's command centre – a point which receives added weight from its close proximity to Carlisle, where recent excavation has shown a continued military presence in the second century, and has revealed evidence for the presence there of detachments at least of all three British legions. Also, as we have seen, a writing-tablet from Vindolanda alludes to the presence at Carlisle of a high-ranking officer, known as a *centurio regionarius*. It has been calculated that the Wall's installations will in all have required around 11,500 men: this will obviously have required some movement of garrisons from existing bases. At present, apart from isolated examples, such as Ribchester, there are few indications of forts affected by such redeployments in the Hadrianic period.

The original purpose of the Wall clearly relates to the observations about security in Britain made in the *Life of Hadrian*. The emperor himself no doubt developed this thinking; to 'separate the Romans from the barbarians' represents a positive attitude to the Romanisation of Britain, which is evident in other likely 'projects' of Hadrian's visit, such as the granting of *civitas*-status to the eastern Brigantes at Aldborough. Without doubt, the technical skill embodied in the structures of Hadrian's Wall and their size and scope were intended to make a clear political statement. This is to be expected of an emperor who well understood the relationship between buildings and politics. We should also, however, bear in mind a more practical purpose; the milecastles of Hadrian's Wall represented fortified gateways through the Wall. Trade passing into or out of the province attracted taxation, and the evidence of Roman material found in Scotland suggests that such trade was heavy: in this context, the Wall prevented uncontrolled movement across the frontier, whilst the milecastles afforded a ready means of collecting such taxes as were due. Thus, Hadrian's Wall fulfilled a number of purposes in the development of Britain as a Roman province. However, in view of the amount of effort which had been expended on it, we need to ask why it was so soon abandoned in favour of the reoccupation of southern Scotland.

A detailed discussion of the Antonine Wall is plainly outside the scope of the present volume;[18] however, some observations on the implications of the new frontier-policy are appropriate. Although the invasion of the Scottish Lowlands took place in A.D. 142–3, it is clear from inscriptions from Corbridge[19] that preparations for it were underway under the governor, Lollius Urbicus, as early as A.D. 139. Many reasons have been adduced for Antoninus' decision; it has been argued that, as a relatively unknown figure (and Hadrian's *second* choice as successor), Antoninus, like Claudius in A.D. 43, needed a major successful foreign-policy initiative to stamp his authority on the empire. Alongside this, it has been suggested that the now-ageing generals of Trajan's reign, disgruntled at what they saw as Hadrian's 'pacifism', were looking for signs of greater dynamism. Against this, however, it should be pointed out that Lollius Urbicus, Antoninus' choice of governor, was in fact a *Hadrianic* protégé.

It is possible that it was now recognised that the 'real' enemies of Roman Britain lay in the north of Scotland, and that, therefore, the frontier as represented by Hadrian's Wall was situated too far to the south. However, some attention should be given to the observations of the Greek writer, Pausanias,[20] confused though they appear to be. Providing a context for Antoninus' forward-move Pausanias relates that the emperor punished the Brigantes for their attack on the 'Genounian region'. Although it is now clear that Pausanias has confused events in Britain with those on the upper Danube, because of the appearance in both places of a tribe with the name, *Brigantes*, we are nonetheless confident that the British Brigantes had been responsible for an upheaval of some kind, the details of which are now lost due to Pausanias' confusion.

It is worth remembering that territorially the northern Brigantes had some reason to feel aggrieved at the effects upon them of the building of Hadrian's Wall. Further, although much of Antoninus' advance into Scotland represented a re-use of Flavian routes and sites, the south-west of Scotland seems to have been an area of particular concern, with new fortifications in Annandale and Nithsdale, and strong defences, in the shape of a multiple ditch-system, given to Birrens. This evidence provides a context for believing that Antoninus did see the need for taking the north-western Brigantes in hand, and policing them properly.

With the building of the new wall in Scotland, Hadrian's Wall was now largely redundant, and it has been convincingly demonstrated through a study of the Samian pottery from the two walls that they were not held contemporaneously.[21] It is clear, for example, that the *vallum*-ditch was filled with turf and its mounds regularly breached to provide ease of passage. It is now widely recognised that some at least of the forts of the

Plate 36. Maryport: The fort.

Plate 37. Beckfoot: The fort. *(Photograph courtesy of Manunair)*

Antonine Wall enjoyed two periods of occupation,[22] and that these two periods have to
be seen within a rather shorter time-span than
previously thought.[23] Our difficulties in reach-
ing a full understanding of these matters, however, spring largely from the unsatisfactory
nature of our source-material; but there are
strong indications that until the early third
century northern Britain remained, spasmodi-
cally at least, a disturbed area.

We have already noticed the need in the
Antonine re-occupation of southern Scotland
to pay particular attention to the south-west.
Fear of such disturbance probably, in part at
least, prompted the decision to extend the
Hadrianic linear frontier westwards from
Bowness-on-Solway along the Cumbrian
coast. The existence of coastal installations
has long been known;[24] however, the questions relating to their extent, complexity,

Plate 38. Biglands House: Milefortlet 1 of the
coastal system. The 'ditch-cordon' is arrowed.
(Photograph courtesy of T.W. Potter)

51

evolution and purpose have been the subject of a great deal of research and debate in recent years.[25] A concentrated period since the mid-1950s of aerial reconnaissance, ground-work and mainly relatively small-scale excavations has revealed the existence on the coastline westward from Bowness-on-Solway of occasional auxiliary forts, fortlets every Roman mile, and two towers between each pair of milefortlets: besides these, there is evidence of linear features in the form of a road with flanking ditches and palisades. Some excavation has taken place at many of the surviving sites, but few have been extensively sampled; these are, Milefortlets 1 (Biglands), 5 (Cardurnock) and 21 (Swarthy Hill) and Towers 2B (Campfield) and 4B (Cardurnock).[26]

The excavations (excluding those at the forts) have generally pointed to three main phases of occupation; further, the excavation on the site of Tower 4B has revealed a development sequence for the coastal defence arrangements which also appear to fall into three phases separated by intervals of disuse.

At that site the first phase was represented by a palisade or fence, fronted (on the seaward side) by a ditch, and having along it, regularly spaced between each pair of milefortlets, small 'platforms' constructed of turf and clay. The second phase consisted of a new palisade, built slightly inland of the first, which cut through the 'platform' of the first phase. This, too, was associated with a road, and was fronted by a re-cut ditch. The third phase had no running barrier, but was represented by a stone-built tower nearer to the sea and overlying the now in-filled ditch.

Features comparable to these have been located further south at Silloth;[27] here there were two palisades, running north–south though not quite parallel to each other, and two ditches which flanked a north–south coastal road. The palisades consisted of a trench packed with clay into which at close intervals double posts had been pushed. It is assumed that these posts supported wattle sections, and that the whole can be seen to fit a description of Hadrianic frontiers to be

Plate 39. Campfield: Tower 2B of the coastal system. (*Photograph courtesy of Manunair*)

Plate 40. Silloth: The palisade. (*Photograph courtesy of G. D. B. Jones*)

found in Spartianus' biography[28] – 'During this period, and frequently at other times, in a great many places where the barbarians are separated off not by rivers but by frontier-barriers, he set them apart by great stakes driven deep into the ground, and fastened together in the manner of a palisade'. This description, which has usually been taken to apply to arrangements in Germany, but which clearly, from the above text, is not meant to be limited to one area alone, can be seen to have obvious relevance to the palisades located on the coast of Cumbria.

How far along the coast similar arrangements exist is hard to say, but it is clear that different areas show evidence of different treatment: for example, running towards Milefortlet 1 (Biglands) from the east, are two ditches which diverge to join the north and south ditches of the milefortlet. It is assumed that these ditches, therefore, provided a corridor in which the coastal installations

were located.[29] Further research, however, has suggested that from Milefortlet 3 (Pasture House), or possibly Milefortlet 2 (North Plain), only a single forward ditch was cut.[30] It is also clear that since Milefortlet 1 (Biglands) is in excess of a Roman mile to the west of Bowness-on-Solway, the two systems (that is, Hadrian's Wall and the coastal system) were not planned in complete conjunction.

The excavation of Milefortlet 1 (Biglands) has demonstrated a sequence of three periods[31] – a sequence which has been shown to be compatible with other milefortlet sites where excavation has taken place. Owing to the sparse nature of the dating evidence, these three periods have to be asserted rather tentatively, apart from the fact that all fall within the second century A.D. It is reasonably certain that phase I should be placed in the period *c*. A.D. 125–140, thus corresponding approximately with the building and first Antonine abandonment of Hadrian's Wall. Given the new, but now generally accepted, sequence on the Antonine Wall,[32] there is no objection to phase II of Biglands being placed between Antonine Wall I and II, with phase III of Biglands commencing *c*. A.D. 163 and extending until *c*. A.D. 180 (or possibly *c*. A.D. 200). At a number of the coastal installations, three phases have been detected, and at none is the dating evidence inconsistent with the chronological model based upon the excavations at Biglands. Further, it is probably not unreasonable to relate the three phases of the milefortlet to the phases recovered at the sites of Towers 2B (Campfield) and 4B (Cardurnock).

The characters of the milefortlets so far examined vary: it would appear that, with the exceptions of Milefortlets 5 (Cardurnock) and 9 (Skinburness),[33] which are larger than average, the areas of the milefortlets are approximately 300–350 square metres in each case – that is, capable of holding a small patrol-group. The larger ones, which housed larger than normal garrisons (perhaps a *centuria*), are probably to be explained in relation to their occupying terminal positions of the two sections in which the coastal system appears to have been conceived – Bowness-on-Solway to Cardurnock, and Skinburness to Risehow.

Although it cannot be said that all of the sites conform to a similar structural pattern, it would appear that most have ramparts of turf and clay, defended by a palisade running on the inner side of a single ditch. At Swarthy Hill (Milefortlet 21), however, excavation has revealed a rampart of less substantial construction, consisting of an inner and outer face of turf containing an infill of earth. They are entered front and rear by six-post timber gateways. The interior buildings are mostly rather unimpressive in appearance, resembling 'sheds' of turf and timber, with cooking facilities. These were presumably the barrack-buildings of the fortlets.

Phases I and II bore a close resemblance to each other, although distinguished by a period of deliberate demolition. Phase III, however, was considerably smaller; the inland gateway appears to have been closed, and the rampart pierced by a single entrance giving on to the coast; this entrance was structurally markedly less impressive than the earlier gateways. Similar deterioration and size-reductions have been observed elsewhere than at Biglands.

The coastal auxiliary forts have similarly produced little firm evidence for the construction-dates and subsequent chronologies. Neither Beckfoot nor Burrow Walls offer any basis for speculation; Moresby, however, has at least produced a building inscription dating to the last decade of Hadrian's reign (A.D. 128–138).[34] A Hadrianic foundation-date has, as a result of the excavations of 1966,[35] been assigned to Maryport, although it is worth pointing our that the evidence of coin-loss at least would support an earlier – perhaps late Flavian – date. Further south, the evidence for Ravenglass is strongly suggestive of a Hadrianic foundation-date – possibly even late in that reign. This evidence might suggest that the whole of the coastal installations were constructed later than Hadrian's Wall, or possibly that, as on Hadrian's Wall itself, the auxiliary forts represent a revision of an earlier plan;[36] neither hypothesis of course precludes the possibility that one fort at least – (that is, Maryport) – predated all the other installations along the coast, or, indeed, that other coastal forts may have had earlier predecessors.

A further problem concerns the overall extent of the coastal installations: the generally accepted enumeration of sites presupposes the existence of a continuous, coherent, 'system' of defences from Bowness-on-Solway, and assumes that they skirted round the bay of *Moricambe* although there is no support in the evidence for this. Indeed, it may be more likely that the defences were conceived in two parts – north and south of *Moricambe*.

The traditional view has been that the southerly extent of the coastal fortifications was to St Bees Head – a view which was thought to have achieved apparent support from the discovery of a possible milefortlet at Harrington Parks,[37] which has a sight of St Bees; the nature of the Harrington site, however, has yet to be determined. Further, the existence of a fortlet, comparable in size to Biglands, beneath the Hadrianic fort at Ravenglass[38] has prompted the suggestion that the system may continue considerably further south than is sometimes supposed. However, a rather stronger argument relies on the changing nature of the coastline south of Maryport, and favours the tower at Risehow as the southern terminus. A compromise may be suggested: it has been shown that the hinterland which is bounded on its southern side by the road from Carlisle to Maryport supported substantial rural settlement. We have seen that in the first half-century of occupation (*c*. A.D. 70–120), care had been taken to protect this area on both its coastal and inland flanks from those who might seek to pillage or destroy. Clearly, this risk grew less severe as the coastline itself began to provide a greater natural defence. Where the cliffs were substantial, an occasional watchtower may have sufficed. We might therefore expect to find further isolated sections of defensive structures where the nature of the coastline merited it, and where the hinterland supported substantial settlement. The lower reaches of the Esk to its estuary at Ravenglass might be regarded as such an area. Further areas could be postulated, and in considering both this and the possibility of sites lost to coastal change, we have to remember that high-tide level on the west coast was considerably higher in the Roman period than it is now.[39]

The purpose of the coastal installations has traditionally been seen in a context of the *military* 'outflanking' of Hadrian's Wall. As suggested above, however, it is perhaps more appropriate to perceive any threat in social and economic terms: the fast-developing agricultural economy of the Carvetii of the Solway Plain encouraged the 'jealous eyes' of neighbours across the Solway who, as we have seen, from events of Antoninus' reign evidently had a potential for unruliness. In any case, it is possible that, if Hadrian's Wall was regarded as a 'tax-and-customs-barrier', some more entrepreneurial figures might attempt to evade their dues by outflanking the Wall.

In short, therefore, we are beginning to see progress on all of the initial questions posed concerning the coastal system – its extent, complexity, evolution and purpose. The first of these requires more work, whilst the other

three, although presenting a clear enough picture for the second century, are further complicated by a limited amount of fourth-century evidence – which we shall consider below (in chapter 7).

The provision of the Stanegate fortifications, then Hadrian's Wall and the coastal system, and then the Antonine Wall, must clearly have necessitated great flexibility in troop disposition in the north. In this matter our lack of detailed chronologies for so many sites severely hampers discussion. It is clear that some of the construction and perhaps garrison duties could be, and were, undertaken by the legions. It is similarly clear that in broad terms the Stanegate forts lost their garrisons when Hadrian's Wall was built, although this cannot be taken as a firm rule, since the *Notitia Dignitatum* in its 'wall subsection' includes Vindolanda,[40] properly a Stanegate fort. Further, we have seen that Hadrian's Wall and the coastal system were not held contemporaneously with the Antonine Wall.[41] These factors will certainly have helped to lend the flexibility necessary for providing garrisons for these frontier arrangements.

Beyond this, relatively little is known in detail of garrison-patterns during the second century. There were certainly movements of legionary detachments both out of and into the province in the middle of the century. Further, it is also known that at some stage in the

Plate 41. Ribchester: Second-century hoard of *denarii*, found in the excavation of 1978.

55

second half of the second century, following Marcus Aurelius' Danube wars, Sarmatian troops were sent to reinforce the garrisons in Britain.[42] At least some of these were in garrison at Ribchester; finds of characteristic eastern metalwork may be pressed into service in an attempt to locate others. On the basis of evidence from the most recent excavations, Papcastle may prove to be one such site. From Hadrian's time onwards, it was a growing practice to supplement the regular legions and auxiliary cohorts and *alae* with irregular units from border areas which are generally known as *numeri* and *cunei*. Of course, for sites where a sufficient body of evidence has been recovered we can sometimes see characteristic fluctuations in the ceramic and numismatic evidence to indicate temporary abandonments or reductions. It is reasonably clear, for example, that Ribchester lost its garrison when Hadrian's Wall was built, as did Lancaster, to facilitate Antoninus' advance into Scotland.[43] Some Pennine forts (such as Castleshaw and Brough-on-Noe) may have lost their garrisons, whilst other forts- (for example, Watercrook) – have provided evidence of relatively complex garrison-patterns, with periods of activity interspersed with periods of apparent demilitarisation.

It has been postulated that a number of sites may have seen reductions or losses of garrisons in the Trajanic/Hadrianic period: for example, Ambleside, Watercrook, Lancaster, Maryport, Kirkby Thore.[44] Further, the evidence of building sequences and of Samian pottery from Watercrook strongly indicates that the fort was being built in stone when the Antonine advance into Scotland began, was then abandoned, and reoccupied following the final withdrawal from Scotland in *c.* A.D. 165. Epigraphic evidence further suggests (in the form of building inscriptions of the governorship of Calpurnius Agricola, A.D. 163–166) that Ribchester and Hardknott[45] were being rebuilt at this stage, from which we might reasonably infer garrison loss or reduction in connection with the second-century frontier movements.

In these few sites for which we have some evidence, we probably see the 'tip of the iceberg' of the Roman army's flexibility. Units could easily be moved: and it is quite likely, in view of the number of very small sites on Hadrian's Wall and the coastal system, and, as is now emerging[46] on the Antonine Wall too, that much of the detailed garrisoning must have been accomplished by taking small detachments from units whose main bases and headquarters' staffs remained elsewhere.

However, the location of troublespots and the assessment of their seriousness remains a hazardous matter, because of the imprecise nature of the source-material; little of it can be pressed to release detail. From the literary point of view, events of the later second century are ill-documented, and coin-loss figures, too (for monetary reasons), become less reliable indicators of occupation patterns. There is some evidence of disturbances amongst the Brigantes, although on what scale is unclear. It would, however, seem excessive to talk of a 'Brigantian rebellion', a term which appears to suggest widespread upheaval. However, it is evident that the first period of occupation of the Antonine Wall ended violently in *c.* A.D. 153–4 – on the basis of the 'dejected Britannia' coin-issue of A.D. 154–5.[49] It is, however, less clear whether the Romans were – albeit temporarily – forced from Scotland, or withdrew from Scotland to meet a threat further south. The evidence of a clustering of coin-hoards[48] does not support the hypothesis of disturbance in the 150s. In any case, the break in occupation of the Antonine Wall was evidently short; indeed, it has been argued that the governor may have reacted too swiftly in withdrawing – only to be ordered back by an emperor whose personal reputation had been closely tied to the Scottish advance.

The reoccupation was short, and had terminated by *c.* A.D. 165, though again the circumstances of termination remain unclear – whether it was due to internal pressures, or whether the development of problems in Europe and the east was leading to a need for troop-redeployment. The final withdrawal from Scotland in c. A.D. 165 (under the new emperor, Marcus Aurelius) was accompanied by at least a partial recommissioning of the installations of Hadrian's Wall and the coastal system, and by some rebuilding of military sites elsewhere in the north. Care, however, needs to be exercised before assuming that such rebuilding was necessarily precipitated by destruction by hostile forces; it could just as well have been due to a programme of repair at forts which had been demilitarised to provide garrisons for Antoninus' forward-policy.

That some level of disturbance, however, continued intermittently in the north through the remainder of the second century cannot be doubted. Commodus' governor, Ulpius Marcellus (A.D. 180–185), had to resist attacks from the north, as is made clear by Dio Cassius, and by Commodus' issue of coins commemorating victory in Britain.[49] Also during Commodus' reign an inscription from Carlisle records the slaughter of 'a band of barbarians' by the Ala Augusta Petriana: further, an undated tombstone from Ambleside[50] records the death of one Flavius Romanus, who was killed by the enemy inside his fort.[51]

The death of Commodus in A.D. 192 ushered in a period of civil war and confusion during which the governor, Clodius Albinus (A.D. 191–196), used elements of the British garrison to further his own ambitions: the result was predictable for we find his successor, Virius Lupus (A.D. 197–201) having to buy off the northern tribes and being heavily involved in rebuilding in the Pennines[52] – whether following destruction or abandonment is hard to say, though the archaeological evidence from Ravenglass[53] certainly supports enemy attack at this time followed by immediate rebuilding. Continuing building work on the frontier and in the hinterland under the Severan governors, Pudens and Senecio (A.D. 202–208), suggests continuing pressure from the north, and the sources indicate that this was despite efforts by the Romans to relieve this pressure by diplomatic initiatives.[54]

The events of the last quarter of the second century seem also to have led, as we have seen, to the decision to abandon most, if not all, of the smaller installations of the coastal system, presumably partly because they were no longer relevant and partly because their manpower may well have been required elsewhere.

Eventually, the pressure developed sufficiently to bring the emperor, Septimius Severus, to Britain in person to lead a new attempt at a solution; the nature of this campaigning, however, makes it clear that by this time, at any rate, the real seat of Rome's difficulties lay in northern Scotland, rather than within the province itself. Severus and his family based themselves at York for what was clearly intended to be the final solution to the long years of disturbance. It is clear that the chief trouble lay north of the Forth/Clyde isthmus, in the shape of the Maeatae, the third-century northern neighbours of Agricola's Caledonii. Severus' campaigns took little, if any, notice of southern Scotland, nor was the Antonine Wall reoccupied. In fact it looks very like Agricola's final campaign repeated on the grand-scale – perhaps hoping to take the heart out of the Maeatae.[55] Severus died at York in A.D. 211 before the work was complete, though his son and successor, Caracalla, did eventually produce a diplomatic solution which, though sneered at by ancient writers,[56] appears to have secured almost a century of peace in the north.

The garrison pattern of north-west England during the third century is difficult to establish without much more excavation:[57] in any case, the ceramic and numismatic evidence provide far less clear indications than they do for earlier periods. We may well expect that the internal upheavals which preceded Severus' rise, coupled with his own great stress on the army as the source of his power, will have led to reorganisation of existing garrisons.

The establishment of peace will have given

the opportunity for more flexible handling (that is, reduction and/or movement) of garrisons. Watercrook, for example, appears to have lost its garrison early in the third century, and to have remained unmanned until the late 260s or early 270s. At Lancaster, there is evidence of substantial rebuilding in the 260s,[58] presumably following a period of abandonment. Indeed, from the Severan period through to the 240s,[59] we find a large number of sites where rebuilding was taking place. As we have seen, although the garrison patterns cannot be recovered in any detail, such evidence as there is, coupled with the

rebuilding activity, strongly suggests large-scale redeployment. Evidently, too, there was now sufficient stability to allow for the withdrawal of garrisons from some parts of the north-west, including at least some of the forts of Hadrian's Wall.

However, as the third century wore on, as we have seen, some remanning took place. It may be assumed that the tensions experienced all over the Empire were beginning to find their expression in Britain also. However, these and other matters relating to the later years of occupation will be treated in the final chapter.

Footnotes

1. *Scriptores Historiae Augustae, Life of Hadrian* 11, 2.
2. Breeze and Dobson, 1976, 54.
3. For more detailed discussions, see Breeze and Dobson, 1976; Breeze, 1982; Shotter, 1996.
4. *RIB* 1051.
5. Hanson and Maxwell, 1983, 59ff.
6. *RIC* II (Hadrian), 577.
7. Potter, 1979, 333f.
8. *JRS* XXXVI (1946), 134ff.
9. *Britannia* XXI (1990), 134ff.
10. Breeze and Dobson, 1976, 52f.
11. Potter, 1979, 321ff.
12. Potter, 1979, 362.
13. Breeze and Dobson, 1976, 43.
14. Austen, 1992.
15. Kilbride-Jones, 1938; Gillam, 1958.
16. Breeze and Dobson, 1976, 48.
17. Hassall, 1976; Shotter in Potter, 1979, 318.
18. Hanson and Maxwell, 1983.
19. *RIB* 1147 and 1148.
20. *Description of Greece* VIII. 43.
21. Hartley, 1972.
22. Breeze, 1975.
23. Shotter, 1976.
24. Bellhouse, 1992.
25. See particularly Higham and Jones, 1975; Potter, 1977; Bellhouse, 1981; Jones, 1982; Higham and Jones, 1985; Bellhouse, 1989.
26. Biglands House (Potter, 1977); Cardurnock (Simpson and Hodgson, 1947); Tower 2B (Jones, 1993); Tower 4B (Jones, 1982).
27. Jones, 1982, 293f.

28. *Scriptores Historiae Augustae, Life of Hadrian* 12.6.
29. Higham and Jones, 1975, 20ff.
30. Jones, 1982, 287.
31. Potter, 1977.
32. Breeze, 1975.
33. Bellhouse, 1954b, 36.
34. *RIB* 801.
35. Jarrett, 1976.
36. Potter, 1979, 359.
37. Jones, 1982, 296.
38. Potter, 1979, 14ff.
39. Jones, 1980; Jones, 1982, 291f.
40. The section on the western empire (40.32ff): the 'Wall' section of the document is of disputed date (Gillam, 1949; Goodburn and Bartholomew, 1976).
41. Hartley, 1972.
42. Dio Cassius, *History of Rome* LXXII. 16 (narrated amongst the events of A.D. 176).
43. Shotter, 1979.
44. See Potter, 1979, 177 for individual references.
45. *RIB* 589 (Ribchester); *RIB* 793 (Hardknott).
46. Keppie and Walker, 1981.
47. *RIC* III (Antoninus), 930; Speidel, 1987.
48. Robertson, 1974, 28ff.
49. Dio Cassius, *History of Rome* LXXIII. 8; for the coins, see *RIC* III (Commodus), 440 of A.D. 183–4.
50. *JRS* LIII (1963), 160.
51. *RIB* 946; cf. *RIB* 2034 and 1142.
52. Hartley, 1980.
53. Potter, 1979, 363.
54. Dio Cassius, *History of Rome* LXXV. 5.

55. Described as a policy of genocide in *British Archaeology* No. 6 (July 1995).

56. Herodian III. 15, 6.

57. See Appendix II.

58. *RIB* 605; see Jones and Shotter, 1988, 208ff.

59. See Appendix III.

6. *The Pax Romana in the North-West*

It was at one time assumed that in the wake of the military conquest of Britain there followed immigration by farmers from Europe anxious to capitalise on the 'rich pickings' to be had in the new province. Such a view was generated partly by the sophisticated organisation which the villa-system of lowland Britain seemed to imply, and partly by the evident luxury of life-style demonstrated by some of the villas. It is now appreciated that the villa-system was a natural development out of the pre-Roman organisation, that many villas were and remained extremely straightforward in style, and that the luxurious villas in general represent a level of wealth achieved by relatively few and only after a considerable period. Further, the observation of the Greek geographer, Strabo (writing in the early first century A.D.), that Iron-Age Britain produced an exportable surplus of grain[1] shows that whilst the architecture of the Iron-Age farm may not have been particularly impressive the methods employed by the farmers clearly were. It is not unreasonable to see these successful Iron-Age farmers as the ruling cliques of their tribes who represented socially and economically the class upon which a system of local government in the new province could be based.

Such a picture is now widely accepted for lowland Britain; farming and other trades were stimulated by the presence of Roman troops who formed a 'market' which required satisfaction, as well as providing physical focal points on which economic and social intercourse were centred. An economic network was thus established which provided the basis for the physical and political organisation of the lowlands once the army moved on.

The Cotswolds offer in microcosm an excellent demonstration: in the early days of conquest, the area was policed through a legionary fortress at Gloucester and an auxiliary fort at Cirencester; together these guarded against any nationalistic activity which might have been based on hill-fort sites, such as Bagendon. Before long, military imperatives were less concerned with this area, and Romanisation began. By the end of the first century A.D. the fortress and settlement at Gloucester was made into a *colonia*, a town high in the Roman urban hierarchy, but by definition largely self-sufficient. The real impact on the social, political and economic landscape was made by Cirencester: after the army moved on (in the early 70s), the civilian settlement which had established itself outside the fort was strong enough as a town to stand on its own feet. It had replaced Bagendon as the focus of local attention, and had developed to the point of being the natural administrative and economic centre of this part of Britain. Those who prospered and who on the basis of their prosperity could be entrusted with the tasks of local government were the descendants of those who in the 40s had used Bagendon and other such sites as the centres of their resistance to the new military occupation.

This in brief is a picture of Romanisation in lowland Britain during the first century A.D.: we need now to compare it with what we know of the north. Even though the close interdependence of Roman and native in lowland Britain has eventually been recognised, opinion has generally been slow to recognize that parts at least of the highland zone can be viewed in a similar way. Attention has been focused on to the predominant military presence, and the native population has been dismissed with such words as 'sparse', 'backward', or 'recalcitrant'. As a result of more excavation of military and non-military sites, of substantial programmes of aerial reconnaissance, and of fresh evidence such as is provided by the Vindolanda writing-tablets, we are now in a much better position to assess

Plate 42. Old Carlisle: The fort and the *vicus* on its southern side, flanking the road from Carlisle to Maryport. (*Photograph courtesy of Manunair*)

the social and economic importance of the military presence in the north, and the relationship that developed between Roman and native in the highland zone;[2] we can begin to see too what level of wealth was achieved by native farmers and, on the analogy of what happened further south, what kinds of responsibilities were entrusted to the rich and influential amongst the local population.

As a crucial part of this discussion we need to assess the changing military imperatives in the area. The 'Roman army' is a term which generates misconceptions both in fact and implication: it conjures up the notion of a ruthless foreign force, bent on the reduction to quiescence and serfdom of the native population amongst whom it worked. However, Rome could not afford to think of her army in that way, for she had not the resources to contemplate an army of the size that would be necessary if all provinces were treated in such a way as to make them seething hotbeds of discontent. In fact, genuine provincial

rebellions against Rome were relatively rare occurrences, indicating that above all things once peace and stability were attained, there was much scope for flexibility of approaches. Tacitus might give the Caledonian chieftain, Calgacus, the dismissive words, 'they create a desolation and call it peace';[3] but it is evident that such would have been decidedly a minority view amongst Rome's subjects. The army was less an instrument of foreign tyranny than a police force whose activities were as much in the interests of local populations as of anyone else.

For economic and political reasons, the Roman army was not allowed to grow endlessly; in fact, over the first two centuries A.D., the average number of troops under arms was approximately 350,000 over the Empire as a whole.[4] Of these perhaps ten percent were committed to Britain – legions and auxiliary troops in approximately equal numbers. Three legions were posted permanently to Britain – VI *Victrix* at York (which in the early

61

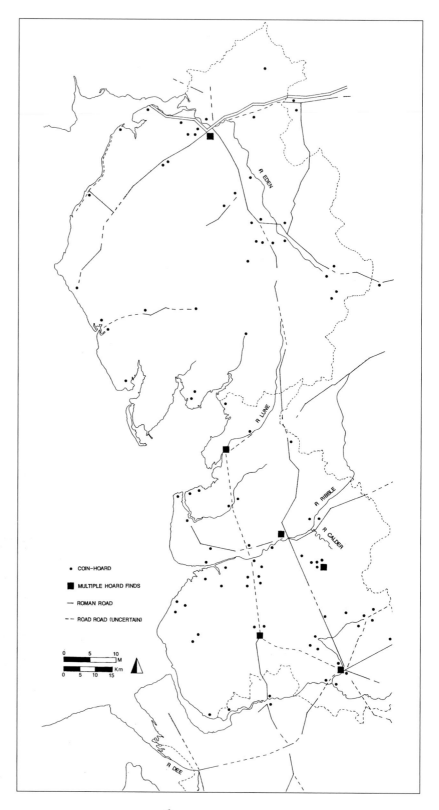

Figure 6.
Findspots of
Romano-British
coin-hoards.

120s replaced IX *Hispana*), II *Augusta* at Caerleon, and XX *Valeria Victrix* at Chester – though these could be used more flexibly with detachments ('vexillations') serving away from their main bases, as clearly happened in the building of the Hadrianic and Antonine Walls in the second century A.D. The legions consisted of 5,500 men each, and were largely made up of infantry; all legionaries were Roman citizens, though this did not of course mean that they were by origin Roman, or even Italian. The deliberate spreading of Roman citizenship through the provinces of the empire meant that large numbers of men from all over the empire were eligible for service in the legions. Thus, in terms of the men who made them up, the legions were diverse units which brought great variety of custom and background to the provinces in which they served. It is likely that in time at least some Britons found their way into the legions, possibly serving in Britain itself.

Serving alongside the legions were units of auxiliary troops; these were organised into smaller groups than the legions – basically 500 or 1000 strong – and could be made up of cavalry (*alae*), infantry cohorts with some cavalry (*cohortes equitatae*), or cohorts which were solely infantry (*cohortes peditatae*). These too could be sub-divided, as clearly happened on the Antonine Wall, where small fortlets were undoubtedly manned by detachments from larger neighbours. Auxiliaries were recruited from amongst those members of the subject-population who were not Roman citizens, and the unit-names – for example, First Cohort of Spaniards – indicate the place of original recruitment. These units were, however, undoubtedly kept up to strength by local recruiting. Their forts made up the policing-network in north-west England, and will have been a dominant feature of the Romanised landscape; their needs, both corporately and individually, served to give shape to the local economies of which they provided the focal points.

The auxiliary units were intended to bring variety to the Roman army, though the general success of Romanisation across the empire meant that they became increasingly similar to the legions. Hadrian introduced a new element of variety into the army by beginning to recruit units of infantry and cavalry of various sizes which we know as 'Irregulars'. These are distinguished from other types of unit by such titles as *pedites* (infantry), *equites* (cavalrymen), *numeri* (detachments), or *cunei* (formations). Little is known of the organisation of these, though some appear to have had specialised skills, such as the '*Numerus Barcariorum*' (detachment of bargemen) who served at Lancaster, and others are recorded in northern forts in the *Notitia Dignitatum*.[5] They seem to have

Plate 43. Maryport: Altar dedicated to Jupiter Optimus Maximus. The inscription reads: 'To Jupiter, Best and Greatest, and to the Divine Spirit of the Emperor, Marcus Maenius Agrippa, the Tribune, set this up'. (*Photograph courtesy of the Senhouse Museum Trust*)

Plate 44. Lancaster: Inscription referring to a third-century rebuilding of the bath-house. The inscription reads: 'For the Emperor [Postumus], on account of the rebuilding of the Bath-house and the restoring from ground-level of the Basilica which had collapsed through old age, for the Soldiers of the Sebosian Cavalry Regiment [Postumus's own], under Octavius Sabinus, Senator and Governor, and under Flavius Ammausius, Prefect of Cavalry: dedicated on 22 August, in the year in which Censor and Lepidus were Consuls, each for the second time'. (*Lancaster City Museum and Art Gallery*)

been housed in existing auxiliary forts, perhaps alongside auxiliary units; one such group was made up of Sarmatian cavalry (from the Danube) who were stationed at Ribchester and were part of a large consignment of such soldiers brought from the Danube following the wars of the emperor, Marcus Aurelius.[6]

All of these troops owed allegiance to the emperor and, through him, to Rome; a group of altars which record the annual oaths of allegiance to Jupiter was found at Maryport, and is now housed in the Senhouse Roman Museum. These altars help to provide information on the garrison-sequence at Maryport, and some were dedicated by a fort commander, Marcus Maenius Agrippa, who was a friend of the emperor, Hadrian. It is upon such altars and other inscriptions and dedications, upon stamped roofing tiles and occasional references in documents, such as the Vindolanda tablets or discharge certificates

(Diplomas) of soldiers, that we are dependent for our knowledge of the disposition and movement of the Roman army in north-west England. Occasionally too finds of metal-work which are characteristic of particular areas of the Empire may offer clues to the nature and identity of units which may have been in garrison at particular forts. For example, as noted above, finds of eastern European metal-work may provide indications of the disposition of more of Marcus Aurelius' Sarmatian irregulars.

After their periods of service the troops of the army were discharged with land and other bounties: legionaries might receive theirs within the context of a town (*colonia*), though frequently auxiliary and irregular troops probably received theirs in the form of small-holdings close to where they had served. In this way, Julius Januarius, a cavalry NCO ('decurion'), appears to have farmed land at Bolton-le-Sands presumably after seeing service at Lancaster.[7] On a larger scale, veterans appear to have made up a significant settlement around the fort at Ribchester. It may well be that in the organisation of land-ownership and tenure in north-west England, some – perhaps, the best – land was appropriated by the authorities for the purpose of veteran-settlement. Obviously, such settlement will have brought constant diversification into the social and economic faces of north-west England.

It is thus crucial that we do not take a blinkered view of the Roman army as a blunt instrument of oppression; as we shall see, it was far more than this, though our ability to look at the army's role in detail is severely hampered by the patchy and inadequate nature of the surviving evidence. From the *Antonine Itinerary*,[8] the *Notitia Dignitatum*[9] and the *Ravenna Cosmography*[10] we have documentation of road-routes, place-names and troop-dispositions (See Appendix IV). But very few place-names are independently attested on inscriptions from sites, which means that road-routes and place-names (and therefore unit-dispositions) are very difficult to fix. The discovery of new sites and new stretches of roads[11] shows that we cannot yet take for granted the general directions of the Itineraries. Further, the fact that we lack detailed chronologies for most sites means that often we do not know even whether particular sites were under occupation when the routes were drawn up. It is thus possible with many of the routes to propose a number of alternative schemes[12] without even then necessarily approaching certainty.

Again, with the *Notitia Dignitatum* which provides a list of sites and military units in the north, we are left with problems of dating and interpretation in the document itself;[13] yet more than this, our lack of knowledge of the place names allows few positive identifications to be made. In any case, few of the inscriptions from the sites themselves, which carry information about garrison-units, can be precisely dated. Thus, too often, although

Plate 45. Lancaster: Rebuilt hypocaust beneath the bath-house.

we know that a certain unit was in garrison at a certain site, we cannot tell when, which means in its turn that we lack the essential data to bring clarity to the *Notitia*. It is, however, clear from surviving documents that units were moved around; for example, the changes of frontier-policy in the second century necessitated much movement. A clear implication of such movements of troops to new bases is that their previous garrison-forts may have been abandoned – even if only temporarily. There is, for example, reasonable evidence to suggest the temporary abandonment of a number of forts in north-west England when Antoninus Pius decided upon the reoccupation of southern Scotland in the 140s.

On the whole, however, we are limited to the most general observations about the garrison-pattern. Following conquest and consolidation the military emphasis clearly moved north in the second century towards

Plate 46. Brougham: Milestone-inscription referring to the Carvetii. The inscription reads: 'For the Emperor, Caesar Marcus Cassianus Latinius Postumus Augustus, Pious and Fortunate, the *civitas* of the CAR(*vetii*).' (*Brougham Castle Museum*)

occurred in the 340s and 380s. Rebuilding in the early fourth century of a number of forts on Hadrian's Wall suggests a remilitarisation of the frontier, and the evidence indicates the retention of a strong military presence well into the second half of the fourth century.

The paucity of evidence makes it hard to study in detail the political, social, economic and cultural impact of the Roman army in the north-west; the generally accepted picture remains heavily dependent upon information derived from a relatively small proportion of available sites. As we have seen, initial resistance to the progress of the Roman army was tough, but by no means universal, amongst the Brigantes. Evidence suggests that some hostility at least was still present in the second century; references in Roman writers support it, and we may assume that the complex frontier movements of the second century represented a response to dangers and threats, continuing into the early third century. Precision is harder to achieve: references to 'Brigantian rebellions' in the second century remain as we have seen, elusive, and at least one – that of Pausanias referring to the reign of Antoninus Pius – may not concern Britain at all. However, an indication of disturbed conditions is provided by the tombstone of Flavius Romanus from Ambleside; with a frankness unusual for a tombstone inscription, Romanus is described as having been killed by the enemy inside his fort.[14] Further, we may begin to wonder whether Roman buildings, which are described as having 'collapsed through old age',[15] may, in fact, have met a more violent end.

the frontiers and their hinterlands. Although the picture is very unclear in the second half of the second century, there must have been renewed attention under Severus and Caracalla in the frontier area, although the successful conclusion of their activities may have allowed a considerable degree of demilitarisation for much of the third century. From the middle of the third century, increasing political instability at the centre meant that troop movements must have been occasioned by the dictates of civil, as well as external, enemies. Britain, for example, was affected by the upheavals of the *Imperium Galliarum* (A.D. 259–273), in which the western provinces separated from the central government; further disturbance took place in the 280s and 290s when Carausius and Allectus ruled Britain separately, and still more such difficulties

Although traditionally we think of the north as 'the military zone', and Roman forts provide a reminder of military imperatives in the area, yet considerable parts of Brigantian territory were apparently handed over to the local people for their administration. In the second century a *civitas* (civil administration) of the Brigantes was established east of the Pennines and centred on the town of Aldborough. Inscriptions from Old Carlisle[16] and Brougham[17] indicate that in the third century the Carvetii, evidently a 'sub-group' of the Brigantes were also 'promoted' to the status of a *civitas*. The administrative centre was presumably at Carlisle, where excavations have not only indicated the extent of the town, but have also provided evidence for substantial structures, such as the large, hypocausted courtyard house in Keays Lane,[18] other substantial buildings in the Lanes area, and the long-lived strip-house at Blackfriars Street.[19] Certainly, on present evidence, Carlisle outstrips other north-west 'towns' in its extent and in the scope of its buildings. How large an area was administered by the Carvetii is harder to say, though it has been suggested that the milestone[20] at Middleton-in-Lonsdale, which marks a distance of fifty-three miles presumably from Carlisle, represents the southern boundary of the tribal *territorium*. There may have been other 'sub-groups' similar to the Carvetii, and it has long been held that Ptolemy's Portus Setantiorum (The Harbour of the Setantii), was situated at the mouth of the Wyre, and was the centre of tribal territory in the Lancashire Fylde. It has, however, to be said that there is as yet no precise clue to the location of the Setantii (see above in chapter 2).

It is at any rate certain that Roman confidence in 'ceding' administrative responsibilities to the Carvetii[21] points to the existence of a class of tribal leaders of suffcient loyalty, wealth and influence to be able and willing to shoulder these responsibilities. In its turn this suggests the development of relationships between local people and Roman administrators, which must have been based on the economic success of local farmers and craftsmen in supplying the needs of the Roman army. It also indicates persuasively that for the most part the relationship that developed between Roman and native was constructive and mutually productive, rather than antagonistic.

Of course, in the early days of occupation the landscape was dominated by the physical signs of conquest and policing – the Roman forts themselves and the roads that linked

Plate 47. Whitley Castle: The heavily-defended fort.

Plate 48. Hardknott: The fort bath-house.

Plate 49. Ravenglass: The fort bath-house.

Plate 50. Manchester: Iron-roasting hearth.

them. If we can draw analogies from other places, the land between the forts will have become the responsibility of the fort commanders. The manner of its treatment will have depended upon a number of factors. For example, areas which had resources of precious metals will probably have been made into imperial estates, and run either directly by the army or by 'trusted' groups treated as lessees. The heavily-defended fort at Whitley Castle probably exercised such a role in the lead/silver industry. Some land will have been taken over by units of the army and used for their own purposes; for example, as can be seen at Hardknott, a considerable area was required for a parade-ground. Land might be taken over by the army for industrial purposes, and particularly in the vicinity of cavalry-forts, extensive areas of grassland may have been cultivated by the army-units

Plate 51. Bowness-on-Solway: A group of local and imported pottery.

themselves. Again, a 'reserve' of land must have been kept for the settlement of discharged soldiers.

Thus, the presence of units of the Roman army had an inevitable and direct effect on landscape-management. However, we should not be misled into seeing this as the 'desolation' attacked so bitterly by Calgacus; the other side of the picture is seen vividly in Dio Cassius' description of the early days of Romanisation in Germany, where the native-population was 'becoming accustomed to hold markets and was meeting in peaceful assemblages'. The Roman army, its needs and infrastructure held clear advantage for people living in the areas which it policed.

The roads themselves, which in the north-west penetrated some very difficult terrain, had advantages for civilians as well as soldiers; the military arterial routes became central features of a growing network of roads which served to link local farmers and industrialists into the Romanised economy. Finds of Roman material – particularly coins and coin-hoards[22] – demonstrate this point clearly. As we shall see, many farmers were left as landowners or tenants to pursue their traditional trades – but now with large new markets to satisfy. However, those most directly affected by the army's presence were the merchants and craftsmen who followed in its wake, and settled outside the forts forming the small towns referred to as *vici*. Such development usually occurred in ribbon fashion along one or more of a fort's access roads (as at Vindolanda), or may, as at Old Carlisle, have focussed on a nearby main road.

There was apparently no standard size, shape or mode of development attaching to *vici*, though to a degree judgement needs to be suspended in view of the small amount of excavation that has taken place on such sites. Most forts in north-west England supported *vici*; only Hardknott appears not to have done, its small extra-mural bath-house servicing a military community alone. Even at the summit of the Stainmore Pass, terracing to the south of the fort at Maiden Castle

Plate 52. Watercrook: An enamelled brooch.

Plate 53. Watercrook: Decorated head of a bone hair-pin.   .

represents artificial platforms provided for the construction of rectangular stone buildings. Clearly the size of the *vicus* would depend on the size and importance of its fort; and a legionary fortress such as Chester, with its 5,500 soldiers, would support much more extensive civilian settlement than an auxiliary fort intended for only 500 troops.

Obviously, however, much will have depended on the importance of an individual fort. Papcastle,[23] for example, a large fort which probably had a key role in the management of security in the interface between the northern Lake District and the good agricultural land of the Solway Plain, seems to have supported an extensive *vicus*; so, too, does Ambleside, presumably because of the

supply-role deriving from its position at the head of Lake Windermere.[24] Aerial photography suggests that *vici* were not planned homogeneously, but developed as the stimulus to do so occurred. They appear to have lacked the prestigious town-centre administrative buildings familiar in the *civitas*-centres of the south – presumably because they did not enjoy any administrative control over their own affairs, but deferred to the fort-commanders.[25] Informal 'associations', however, did occur, as is shown by a dedication to the god, Vulcan, made by the *Vikani* (townspeople) of Vindolanda,[26] and such associations might have formed the basis for some limited local administration.[27] Some *vici* appear to have been relatively densely settled, whereas others, generally referred to as 'dispersed *vici*', were rather more like occasional small settlements on the roads leading out of a fort (as at Brougham). It is generally assumed that *vici* did not have defensive walls, although, at Ribchester, excavation has revealed traces of a defensive rampart and ditch apparently enclosing the settlement. The interpretation of this feature is still unclear, although it is possible that Ribchester may have constituted a 'special case', because of retired soldiers being settled in the *vicus* – as the Roman name BRESNETENACI VETERANORVM seems to imply.[28]

In many cases, *vici* appear to have begun development very soon after the establishment of a fort;[29] buildings initially, as at Watercrook, were of timber, but were in most cases converted to stone later. Typical of these buildings were long, narrow, structures with their gable-ends facing on to the street. These buildings had internal divisions which may have provided for a shop on the street frontage, with living accommodation behind and perhaps a 'yard' at the rear where the resident family (or families) engaged in producing goods which could be offered for sale in the shop. In most cases access to individual rooms was not provided by an independent corridor but had to be gained by proceeding through one room to another.

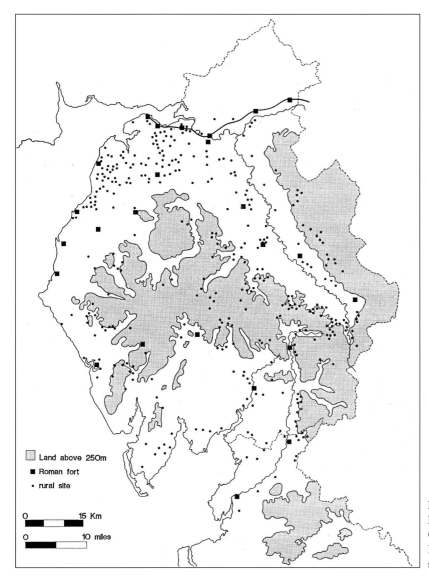

Figure 7.
Rural sites in
Cumbria and
North Lanca-
shire.

Only if neighbouring buildings, which would normally be separated by a narrow alley-way, came under single ownership could the alley be roofed to provide an internal corridor.

Inhabitants of such buildings may have been traders or craftsmen attracted over long distances[30] by the market which the fort represented, though most of those who lived in the *vici* were probably more local in origin: many young women, for example, may have been attracted by unofficial liaisons formed with serving soldiers which could be for-

malised into marriage after a soldier's demobilisation. From the time of Septimius Severus, however, soldiers were allowed to marry whilst still serving.

Although we have little direct evidence of the nature of *vicus*-populations, it appears likely that they were diverse in nature and origin, though linked by their common ability to provide something which soldiers needed. Undoubtedly, many craftsmen were attracted by the opportunities, and a number of *vici* have provided evidence of industrial activity

Plate 54. Vindolanda: 'Strip-building'.

in the form of furnaces, weaving equipment, kilns, tanning pits as well as waste products from many processes.[31] Metal-working will obviously have occupied a major place in the industrial life of the *vici* in order to facilitate repairs of military and civilian property, and to produce a wide range of tools, utensils, fittings and decorative items. Much of this was probably organised on an individual basis, though the *vicus* which lay to the north of the fort at Manchester[32] had a considerable area devoted to furnaces, housed apparently in sheds and 'lean-to' structures, which might justify its description as an 'industrial estate'. It is not surprising that Vulcan, the patron-deity of metal-workers, is the object of a dedication found in the *vicus* at Vindolanda.

In the early days of the *vici* at least, the military and civilian communities will have depended upon local potters to supplement the supply of vessels which could be acquired from other sources. In some cases, the need for a range of terracotta products – tiles and bricks as well as pottery – was such that

military units themselves might in a location adjacent to a good supply of suitable raw materials establish an industrial complex, as happened at Quernmore (near Lancaster). Fine wares, such as the red-glazed samian pottery, were imported from Europe, and were presumably sold by travelling salesmen to local shops for selling-on to individuals. In course of time, the supply of such basic products appears to have been organised on a far larger scale with substantial military contracts beings placed with manufacturers in various parts of the country; for example, the British fine-ware known as 'colour-coated' was manufactured in very large quantities in the Nene Valley; black and grey cooking-pots were made in various centres in southern England. In the north-west, large industrial sites, sufficiently well organised to handle substantial contracts developed at such places as Heronbridge, Stockton Heath and Wilderspool (see below).

There will have been plenty of work for joiners in the *vici*, particularly when many of the buildings will have been constructed of timber, and when much repair work of wooden structures and vehicles will have been necessary. Joiners' tools have often been found, and they of course will have constituted an important product for the metalworker. Nor should we forget that the timber used by the joiner as his raw material and by other tradesmen for the firing of furnaces presupposes the availability of local supplies which could have been kept up only by a sophisticated programme of woodland management.[33]

This serves to emphasise the relationship between fort and *vicus* on the one hand with the adjacent countryside on the other. In no sense, however, will this relationship have been more crucial, as the Vindolanda writing-tablets indicate, than in the supply of food to the forts and to individual traders. It goes without saying that local farmers will have geared their activities not only to supply their own families and satisfy the taxman, but also to produce a surplus to be sold. Such products must have taken account of the tastes of the market; for example, studies of butchered bones indicate that optimum ages for slaughter were recognised and observed.[34] One site at Vindolanda has been identified as a likely butcher's-shop because of its counter and the provision of an internal drain linked to the main sewer outside in the street.[35] In all, a wide variety of food products was undoubtedly sold in *vicus*-shops, and perhaps in many cases precooked to be sold as 'take-away' meals. Similarly, we may assume that local farmers were well prepared to provide hides and fleeces for the manufacture in the *vici* of shoes and clothes, although in the case of hides some might be taken by the authorities as tax for the manufacture of tents.

Thus, the available evidence points not only to a vibrant trading-situation in the *vici*, but also close relationships between the *vicus*-traders and the wider tribal community. There were, of course, many other services available in the *vici*. We may, for example, with confidence postulate a 'leisure-industry'

in the form of bars, restaurants, and brothels. The bath-houses provided, under official auspices, the closest equivalent that the Roman world had to our 'leisure-centres', and often provided both for soldiers and civilians not simply bathing facilities, but also a range of other relaxation-activities. Because of its crowded nature, the bath-house was not just a major social centre, but could also provide 'cover' for criminal activities too. Again, the constant heating of water required in the bath-house emphasises the need for large timber supplies in the area adjacent to the *vicus*.

Our knowledge of *vici*, fragmentary though it is, provides evidence of other structures and services. Some may have contained

Plate 55. Maryport: Celtic horned deity. (*Photograph courtesy of the Senhouse Roman Museum Trust*)

Plate 56. Carlisle: Dedication to Mars Ocelus and the Imperial Cult (*Carlisle Museum and Art Gallery*). The inscription reads: 'To the god, Mars Ocelus, and to the divine spirit of the Emperor [...] Augustus'.

a 'hotel' (*mansio*), a large building consisting of rooms arranged around an open courtyard, with its own bath-house and stables. This provided a basic level of accommodation for official travellers, particularly the couriers of the imperial post. It is quite likely that evidence of a small bath-house forming part of a large courtyard building recognised to the north of the fort at Lancaster indicates a *mansio* at that site – unless it be part of an official residence belonging to an important official, such as the tax-official known as a *beneficia-rius consularis*, known to have been at Lancaster.[36]

The evidence of surviving inscriptions indicates that a wide variety of religious practices will have been catered for in the *vici* – though not necessarily all contemporaneously. Traditionally, Romans and the Romanised Celtic peoples of the west were superstitious, and looked to divine help and protection in a wide variety of activities. Because of this, religion had always proved to be a powerful political weapon, since the authorities, in their priestly roles, could advise people on action that needed to be taken to keep the gods happy. In Britain, Roman and Celtic divinities were able to come into close relationship: both communities were polytheistic and both saw their gods as presiding over particular activities. These were often brought together in the so-called *interpretatio Romana*, in which a Roman and equivalent Celtic deity were effectively 'fused' into one – for example, *Apollo Maponus* at Ribchester, *Mars Ocelus* at Carlisle, and *Mars Cocidius* at Bewcastle. It enabled the Roman authorities to cause little disturbance to existing beliefs, except perhaps to organise them in a more formal way. For example, at Carrawburgh (on Hadrian's Wall), where in the pre-Roman period a natural spring was regarded as the manifestation of the goddess, Coventina, the spring was enclosed in a concrete basin and housed in a square 'Romano-Celtic' temple. Dedications to Coventina also show how she came to be perceived in anthropomorphic form.

Certain religious observances were required officially. Although most Roman emperors did not view themselves as gods, their extraordinary position in society was marked by the 'imperial cult' in which an obligatory demonstration of political loyalty was channelled through the observance of their 'divine spirit' (*numen*). Numerous surviving altars and dedications record such statements of loyalty on the parts of units of the Roman army, and of other groups and individuals. As head of the Roman pantheon, Jupiter, the

Plate 57. Ribchester: Dedication to Apollo Maponus. The god is depicted in the classical lyre-playing pose (*citharoedus*) (*Ribchester Museum*)

Plate 59. Kirkham: Altar to three Mother-goddesses.

Plate 58. Papcastle: Bronze statuette of Marsyas. (*Photograph courtesy of Lancaster University Archaeological Unit*)

Greatest and Best (*Jupiter Optimus Maximus* or *IOM*), received especial attention as a focus of political interest; individuals might purchase small statuettes of emperors or of official Roman gods to place in their own homes as indications of their own loyalty. Of course, these statuettes, such as the Manchester Jupiter, constituted for metal-workers and potters products for which the market would never dry up.

Particular groups and individuals would see divine associations of particular relevance to themselves; the army, for example, would look to Mars and Hercules, and sometimes brought these to Britain in forms familiar to them in their own countries of origin. Thus, a unit of Germans at Housesteads put up a dedication to *Mars Thincsus*. Others might equate Mars with a deity native to Britain, such as *Mars Cocidius* (at Bewcastle). Metal-workers sought the especial protection of the smith-god, Vulcan, whilst musicians

Plate 60. Bewcastle: Silver plaque dedicated to the Celtic god, Cocidius: the god probably gave his name to the site – *Fanum* ('shrine') *Cocidi.*

might look to Apollo. A dedication stone from Ribchester to *Apollo Maponus* portrays the god with his lyre, and an apparent temple-site at Papcastle produced a bronze statuette of the satyr-figure, Marsyas, who was worsted by Apollo in a music-contest, and then flayed alive for his temerity in having issued a challenge to the god of music. These might indicate the presence of guilds of musicians in some of the *vici* in support of local ceremonial.

There are also examples of local deities becoming Romanised, but not equated with a Roman god. Thus the spring-goddess, Coventina, presumably guaranteed water-supplies at Carrawburgh, whilst Ialonus (perhaps the deity of the river Lune at Lancaster) was invoked by an ex-soldier, presumably to bring health to his crops. In a similar way, the protection sought for the well-being of a town or tribe could be channelled through a personified tutelary deity; a relief-carving of the goddess *Brigantia* which was found at Birrens represented the tutelary deity of the

Brigantes in the classical form of a winged victory figure. Similarly a small stone bust from Carlisle, depicted wearing a 'gated' crown, was the tutelary deity of this town of the Carvetii.

In addition to these official and semi-official deities, the forts and *vici* of the northwest have provided ample evidence of non-Roman 'mystery' cults – such as Sun-worship, Mithraism, Isis-worship and, of course, Christianity. These cults, which, unlike the state cults, were practised in the secrecy of their temple-buildings, mostly originated in the eastern Mediterranean and found their way to Britain through the movements of soldiers and merchants. They became more popular because they offered a hope to the individual of salvation from and a 'personal relationship' with a god, which were not essentially features of the state cults. They were tolerated so long as they did not encourage conflict; the Roman objection to Christianity was based upon the refusal of Christians to render their obligations to the state cults.

The secrecy attaching to most of these cults prevents our knowing a great deal about them, and generally they appear to have enjoyed intermittent observance at particular places – presumably because they needed the authority and financial resources of a senior person – (for example, a fort commander) – to lead them. There may also have been an element of fashion and political expediency attaching to such cults, as is presumably the case with the dedication at York early in the third century A.D. to the Egyptian god, Serapis, at the time when York provided the base for the emperor, Septimius Severus, and his family who were themselves devotees of the cult.

Few temples dedicated to these cults survive: their presence is generally attested by inscriptions or cult-objects. The most tangible evidence is provided by the cult of the Persian god of light, goodness and truth, Mithras, who attracted interest amongst both soldiers and merchants. The best-preserved Mithraic temple in Britain is the small rectangular

Plate 61. Carrawburgh: Temple of Mithras.

Plate 62. Carrawburgh *Mithraeum*: Altar group. The altar on the left is pierced through so that the light from a lamp could shine through Mithras' radiate sun-crown.

building situated off the south-west corner of the fort at Carrawburgh. It had four separate periods of use between the mid-second and early-fourth centuries when it was finally destroyed violently, probably at the hands of Christians who regarded the Mithraic liturgy as a kind of 'devilish' version of their own. The temple has a central nave, which would have been dominated by the highly colourful relief of Mithras slaying the primeval bull and allowing its blood and semen to soak into the earth and to become the source of life and fertility for mankind. The nave was flanked by 'aisles' on which were situated benches on which initiates could recline during the ritual meal. Separated from this was an ante-chamber where would-be initiates may have been 'tested' before being allowed into the sanctum. It is likely that the atmosphere was 'heady', due to the burning of pine-cones and the very restricted lighting, of which one feature survives – an altar depicting Mithras wearing the sun-ray crown on which the rays have been pierced through so that a light placed at the back of the altar could shine through them.

Although no other Mithraic temples have been found in the north-west (except at Housesteads, also on Hadrian's Wall), various sites have produced Mithraic sculptures – Chester, Manchester, Maryport and possibly Lancaster, too, where one piece in a hoard of sculpture found in the late-eighteenth century has Mithraic features.

The evidence for Christianity in the forts and *vici* of the north-west is less promising than for other religions. Christianity was, until Constantine's Edict of Milan of A.D. 312, a forbidden religion; this meant that the activities of Christians until then had to be conducted covertly. Even after A.D. 312, the administrative classes of the empire were slow to renounce traditional paganism. The surviving evidence all consists of individual items, from which generalisations cannot readily be drawn; no certain Christian structure survives from the late Roman period in the north-west. Yet it is likely that during the

fourth century at least there must have been converts, and groups of Christians will have gained in confidence.

The earliest evidence for Christianity in the north-west is provided possibly by a fragment of amphora-wall from the *vicus* at Manchester; this fragment was inscribed with part of a 'word-square', in which the re-arranged letters give the words PATER NOSTER (twice) with two spare As and Os, The words PATER NOSTER of course mean 'Our Father' and the letters of the square allow them to be arranged in a cruciform fashion; the letters 'A' and 'O' are Latin rendering of the Greek letters 'alpha' and 'omega' ('the beginning' and 'the end'), which were themselves often used as a Christian cryptogram.[37] The context of the Manchester example is mid-second century A.D., although it has to be said that, as with the similar example from Cirencester, not all authorities are agreed that such word-squares do in fact necessarily have a Christian significance.

Three tombstones from the north-west betray indications of Christian burials; two (one each from Carlisle and Brougham) – employ the formula which indicates that the deceased person lived for 'x years more or less'.[38] The vagueness was an indication of the relative unimportance of the length of time spent on earth. The third – from Maryport – is a fragment which contains the Christian cryptogram, *chi-rho*, the first letters in Greek of 'Christos'.[39] For the rest, personal objects such as lamps and finger-rings are the only indications of Christian owners. A recent discovery with a great deal of potential for understanding the role of the early church in the lives of the people is a salt-pan found near Crewe.[40] This bears an inscription which suggests that the church may have played an organisational role in the salt-industry, akin to that which is much more familiar in the context of the medieval monastic church.

It has been suggested that unusual church-dedications may offer a clue to the locations of early Christian communities: in this case, a dedication to St. Elphin – (Romano-British

Plate 63. Carlisle: A possible Christian tombstone. The inscription reads: 'To the Spirits of Underworld: Flavius Antigonus Papias, a Greek, lived for sixty years, *more or less*, and returned to the Fates his soul which had been lent to him for that period of time'. (*Carlisle Museum and Art Gallery*)

name, Alphinus) – at Warrington may be of significance. Beyond this, any pre-Conquest Christian evidence may conceal the existence of Romano-British Christian centres. Thus, the church-sites at Heysham Head, Urswick and Aldingham may be of interest in this connection.

A further aspect of Romanised town-life was entertainment and ceremonial. Traditionally, gambling was popular and was undoubtedly carried on widely in bars and on pavements. Evidence of board-games – (possibly of the war-game type) – has been found in the north-west in the shape of a 'board' made of stone, and crudely divided up into squares, and of a large collection of bone counters which was located in a barrack-area at Ravenglass.[41] The stone-built amphitheatre at Chester[42] provides evidence of more organised entertainment and ceremonial. Such sites were obviously relevant in the context of the large military and civilian population to be expected of a legionary fortress, but smaller versions may have been located close to other fort and *vicus* sites in the north-west. A pottery face-mask found at Wilderspool[43] may offer a clue to the type of entertainment provided, whilst a vivid indication of military ceremonial is provided by the Ribchester parade-helmet. Partly because of their size, amphitheatre sites were normally situated at the edges of settlements, as is the case with those at Chester, Caerleon and Cirencester although it may also be relevant that, in Roman eyes, a town-boundary represented the dividing-line between 'civilisation' and 'untamed nature'; it would thus provide a suitable location for a building which was so often the scene of an enacted struggle between life and death. In some parts of the country – as at Dorchester – there is evidence of the 'conversion' of henge-monuments of suitable size to this purpose.

As we have seen, some of the surviving

evidence of Christians in Roman north-west England consists of tombstones which contain the use of formulae of possible Christian significance. Few of the north-west's cemetery sites are known with any certainty. Roman law forbade the placing of any burials (except for those of infants) within settlement areas, and it was normal practice for the roads leading out of towns to be lined with tombs. Thus evidence has come from Penny Street in Lancaster of cremation urns, confirming that that street represents the likely line of a Roman road heading through the *vicus* and continuing along the southern side of the river Lune. Further south, some two miles out of Lancaster (at Burrough Heights), a rectangular earthwork has been located by the side of the Roman road which has been tentatively identified as a substantial roadside mausoleum.[44] However, the most significant cemetery evidence has come from a site approximately three-quarters of a mile to the south of the fort at Low Borrow Bridge and flanking the eastern side of the road. Evidence has come to light of approximately sixty cremation urns and a few inhumations, which appear to have been arranged in sub-rectangular or circular plots which were perhaps distinguished by low hedges or fences. One complete tombstone recovered from the site records the death of the age of thirty-five of Aelia Sentica; the stone was erected by her husband, Aurelius Verulus.

The *vicus* provided an incentive for craftsmen to come and set up business: they may even have been officially encouraged to bring

Plate 64. Salt-pan with a possible Christian name on it. A possible interpretation of the 'inscription', which is at the top of the photograph, is 'Belonging to Viventius, the Bishop'. (*Photograph courtesy of Cheshire Museums Service*)

themselves within the organised scope of these sites. The *vici* were not, however, the only sources of manufactured goods available to the north-west's population. Besides the influx of goods from other parts of Britain and even the continent, we have evidence of local industrial sites, some of which were undoubtedly directly controlled by the army.

The most completely known of the military depots in the north-west is the one at Holt in Denbighshire, which serviced the legionary fortress at Chester.[45] The depot was producing tiles and pottery from the late first century into the third, with the peak of activity in the first half of the second. The twenty-acre site produced evidence of 'barracks', a building interpreted as an officer's house, and a bath-house – in addition to the industrial buildings themselves. It is similarly possible that the impressive buildings located at Walton-le-Dale, a site which contains hearths and wells, should also be interpreted as belonging to a legionary depot; the date-range of these, too, appears to be late first to early third century.[46]

Besides these major military depots, smaller (presumably auxiliary) depots have been located: Muncaster presumably supplied Ravenglass and Hardknott,[47] Scalesceugh perhaps Carlisle and Old Penrith; in addition a large tilery was discovered at Brampton;[48] both of these were operating in the early-second century, and should perhaps be connected with the development of the Stanegate *limes*. The Brampton works, which saw the largest examination of all such sites in the north-west, was observed to be of markedly inferior construction compared to the legionary equivalent at Holt. It is thought that in the case of Brampton, the depot was sufficiently close to Old Church fort for the living accommodation to have been provided there. Two further sites of this type, approximately a mile apart, but on the same contour, have been located at Quernmore, some three miles east of Lancaster;[49] at one a crudely constructed tile kiln and a better pottery kiln, together with evidence for iron-working, were located, and thought to fall within the

date-range of *c.* A.D. 80–160. No evidence of administrative buildings was recovered.

Excavations at both Quernmore and Lancaster have put the connection of the two sites beyond question: die-linked stamps of the *Ala Sebosiana* have been recovered at both, and analysis of the clays has confirmed the connection. It should, however, be noted that fragments of hollow voussoir tiles[50] recovered from the sub-floor debris of the third-century bath-house were found to bear no relationship to the Quernmore material. Since these must post-date the mid-third century rebuilding (*RIB* 605), it confirms the impression that the local tilery was no longer in operation and that supplies must by that time have been organised on a different basis.

The close approximation of dates from sites of this nature suggests that their phasing-out was an act of policy, and presumably reflects two things: first the main phases of building of military sites were complete and repair work would (hopefully) not require building-materials on such a scale. Second, larger mass-producing sites elsewhere in the country were presumably by that time (that is, late-second/early-third centuries) well able to cope with the demands made of them. This is obviously true of pottery, where the bulk of the military market in the later second century was being serviced by east Gaulish Samian, black-burnished products from Dorset, and Nene Valley ware.

Industrial activity, mainly iron- and salt-working, has been noted at a number of

Plate 65. Chester: The Amphitheatre.

81

Plate 66. Low Borrow Bridge: The cemetery-site. The site shows many phases of sub-rectangular and sub-circular burial-plots. (*Photograph courtesy of Lancaster University Archaeological Unit*)

Plate 67. Low Borrow Bridge: Cremation-urn. (*Photograph courtesy of Lancaster University Archaeological Unit*)

Cheshire sites: extensive evidence for metal working, together with a widespread area of sheds and workshops has been revealed at Heronbridge,[51] ranged on both sides of Watling Street and close by the Dee, a little south of Chester. Activity seems to have continued here from the late-first into the third century, although it is not clear whether the site was 'private' or run upon military lines. A similar doubt hangs over Northwich, Middlewich, Whitchurch and Nantwich, all of which have yielded abundant evidence of industrial activity. Conceivably this originated in the context of a *vicus*, since the first three sites had military phases. It may well be, however, that when military occupation came to an end, the industrial activity, presumably in the hands of civilians, was able to continue.[52]

Finally, at the point where the road from Northwich to Walton-le-Dale crosses the Mersey, is situated the most extensive of the north-west's industrial sites – at Wilderspool and Stockton Heath. The site, which apparently, as at Heronbridge, straddles the road,

Plate 68. Walton-le-Dale: Foundation-trenches for large sheds.

has seen a number of extensive excavations,[53] the largest being at the turn of the present century. Many different industrial activities have been recognised – working in iron, bronze and lead, pottery, tile- and glass-making, as well as enamelling.

The site is criss-crossed with fence-posts and ditches, which are presumably property demarcations, though the latter could conceivably be water-channels. A few stone buildings have been located, but the majority are of timber construction; whilst most are basically rectilinear, a circular one located in the excavations of 1976 gives rise to speculation about the nature of the inhabitants. Such a building strongly suggests a native British origin, and it has been suggested that the 'trade-mark' type of mortarium-stamp might in fact simply represent illiterate blundering, rather as occurs on copies of Roman third-century radiate coins.[54]

The products of the Wilderspool pottery-kilns have been traced in many parts of the north-west, and as far north as the Antonine Wall. Although a putative set of 'defences'

Plate 69. Wilderspool: an area of the site showing fence-lines, aqueducts and (at the rear) foundations of a circular hut.

has often been assumed to represent the remains of a Flavian fort, neither the nature of these features nor the dating-evidence recovered from the site is in fact consistent with such an assumption, though the possibility remains of an early fort in the vicinity.[55] Indeed, in common with other 'industrial' sites, occupation appears to have been principally from the end of the first century A.D. until early in the third, although a scatter of later material[56] indicates that some form of activity continued at Wilderspool into the fourth century. There is also evidence from Wigan which would appear to be consistent with a site of an industrial nature.[57]

The nature of sites like Wilderspool, Heronbridge and the industrial areas of the *vici* suggests that the workers were principally native craftsmen who for one reason or another (voluntarily or under persuasion) came into the organised areas to work – perhaps to secure a better hold on the assured markets which the Roman occupation offered. Some, however, like those of the Craven Caves in Yorkshire, perhaps preferred independence and proximity to their raw materials.[58]

The bulk of the population, we can assume, remained as they had long been – arable farmers and pastoralists. However, the lack of excavation of rural sites in north-west England leaves much doubt as to the nature of the relationship between farmers and the populations of the forts and *vici*. There are in fact many questions about the nature of the rural economy to which the answers in the present state of our knowledge can be no more than provisional.

Outwardly, the most striking difference between the rural economies of the highland and lowland zones is the absence from the former of structures which are classified as villas. The villa-estate of the lowland zone represented a level of architectural Romanisation in the countryside, and existed alongside rural sites whose nature and appearance are much closer to those found in the north-west; the villa-estate also assumes a certain level of affluence in terms of land and finance.[59] It is clearly too crude an assumption to argue that because the north-west generally lacked villa-estates, its farmers also lacked land and finance, for the establishment of the *civitas* of the Carvetii in northern Cumbria clearly does assume a strong level of wealth amongst its leaders; it is difficult to imagine a source of that wealth other than agriculture.

The north-west has so far yielded two sites which conform to the description of a villa as measured by the criteria used in the lowland zone – Eaton-by-Tarporley (near Chester) and Kirk Sink (near Skipton).[60] There may of course be more to locate, but such a small number may be explained by the movement of a small number of individuals from further south. The vast majority of rural sites in the north-west are made up of circular and sub-rectangular structures in complexes of varying size and constructed either of stone or of timber. Clearly, such complexes consist of both domestic sites and fields or yards. Our knowledge of the distribution of such sites suggests that some were small farms whilst others may well have been the centres of estates of considerable size.

Such study as has taken place indicates that we cannot employ simple criteria such as chronological development or level of Romanisation to explain the differences in shape and building materials. Indeed, artefactual evidence indicates no obvious distinctions in date or ownership, whilst the difference in building materials appears to represent the use of timber on sites located in the valleys with stone used mainly on sites at higher altitude, as at Maiden Castle-on-Stainmore. This in its turn probably does no more than reflect the process (human and environmental) of deforestation. It is clear, too, that some at least of the rural sites of all types enjoyed long histories, stretching back beyond the Romano-British period (as at Ewe Close in the Upper Lune Valley or Urswick 'stone walls') and continuing much later (as at Gauber High Pasture in Upper Ribblesdale).[61]

There can be no doubt that the presence of the Roman army with its dependent populations in the *vici* will have opened up considerable opportunities for those involved in agriculture – tastes in food and drink to be accommodated, as well as openings into the 'textile-market', and the provision of hides for tents and for transforming into leather goods, and the rearing of working-animals and fodder for them.

As well as this, whilst most metal and

mineral resources will have been officially handled, some scope was probably left for local extraction and profit. Some of these products will have been taken by way of taxation, but farmers and landowners in the north-west will have been left sufficient for their own needs, and many will have had a surplus which could be sold for profit. It is a reasonable assumption that most of those involved in the rural economy will soon have come to appreciate what the market required; as we have noticed already, it is clear that animals reared for meat will have been slaughtered at an 'optimum age'.

How the land was distributed must remain a matter for conjecture, but some must have been appropriated by the authorities for the settlement of discharged soldiers, and it may be assumed that this was likely to have been the land of better quality, such as was situated in coastal areas and in the valley-floors. Although the evidence remains inconclusive, it was long ago conjectured that land on the Fylde may have been used for veteran settlement, and it is highly likely that the veterans of Ribchester, as well as enjoying a stake in the *vicus*, had allotments of land in the Ribble Valley. One piece of evidence which may be significant is the altar set up near Bolton-le-Sands by Julius Januarius who described himself as a retired decurion – presumably from the fort at Lancaster. Preferential treatment

Plate 70. Colt Park (Upper Ribblesdale): Romano-British farm, showing a circular hut in the foreground (with an entrance on the right) and field/plot boundary-walls.

in the quantity and quality of land distributed will have been afforded to veterans of the legions, of auxiliary cavalry units, and of auxiliary infantry in descending order. It has been suggested that land designated for such use might show signs of centuriation,[62] the traditional Roman form of land distribution, though at present no certain evidence of this practice has been located.

Despite such imperatives, however, it is unlikely that the authorities were insensitive to the needs and aspirations of Brigantian farmers. Thus much land-tenure and usage was probably left without interference, for it was by the middle of the first century A.D. generally held by the Roman emperor and his advisers that local populations were generally easier to manage if left to pursue traditional activities and methods. Also, it can be shown that the belief existed that native populations could advance themselves socially and politically if the profitability of their activities was encouraged. Although the period of Roman occupation may not have led to striking advances in agricultural technology, and although uncontrolled deforestation could obviously not be allowed, the clearance of some land will have greatly enhanced the opportunities for profit-making.

Two factors have been amply demonstrated: first, we clearly have to reject the notion, often advanced in the past, that apart from the areas of the Roman sites themselves, the population of the north-west was thin.[63] Secondly, it is clear from the locations of agricultural sites that there must have been a strong economic inter-dependence between the Roman and native populations, a point also effectively confirmed by the 'stores-lists' preserved in the Vindolanda tablets.[64]

The plotting of sites has proceeded much further in Cumbria than in Lancashire; conditions in the latter do not readily lend themselves to aerial research;[65] thus the number of known sites is small, although finds of Roman material suggest that the Roman roads and the river valleys will have provided the chief foci for settlement. Nonetheless,

Plate 71. Castle Hill, Leck: Romano-British farm. (*Photograph courtesy of Lancaster University Archaeological Unit*)

possible traces of the Romano-British landscape have been observed on the eastern flank of the West Lancashire mosses; and there are signs that the higher ground in the Fylde may have supported settlement.[66]

North of Lancashire, considerable settlement has been observed on the limestone of the Ribblehead area, as at Gauber High Pasture and Colt Park.[67] In north Lancashire and Cumbria, the principal areas of settlement are located in the valley floors and slopes of the communications corridors provided by the Lune and Eden rivers, and again on the Solway Plain and the northern slopes of the Lake District.[68]

Although excavation of rural sites has been very limited, it would appear a reasonable assumption that a high proportion of them, even if multi-period, was active in the Roman period. It is similarly reasonable to suppose that many, if not most, of the sites, both arable and pastoral, enjoyed an 'economic relationship' with the Roman forts and *vici*.

In other words, they were producing grain surplus to their taxation-requirement, and their animal husbandry was to an extent organised to take account of the Roman market for meat.[69]

Environmental characteristics were clearly the chief limiting factors to the farmer's activity; in particular, deforestation and soil erosion will have limited the use to which the higher terrain – that is above approximately 1000ft – could be put. At the same time the very process of soil erosion from higher levels will have led to enhanced fertility in the valleys. During the Roman period, deforestation by environmental causes was intensified by the need for timber for building, though in a number of places excavation has revealed that Roman forts were being built in areas already without forest cover, having been given over to grassland or occasionally to ploughing. Deforestation will have affected not only the local farmer's use of the land, but also the materials he used to provide housing for himself. Clearly, stone would have had to be used where timber was in short supply. Thus, for that reason, if for no other, the higher rural settlements would tend to be stone-built – and, incidentally, more resilient to the passage of time. Timber, wattle and thatch were generally used at lower levels, though a circular hut at Fingland appears to have been constructed of turfs laid on a stone foundation.[70]

A total picture is of course beyond recovery; particularly in the valley floors and on the lower slopes subsequent agricultural activity has destroyed a good deal of the evidence. However, the density of sites located, particularly on the good land of the valley floors, suggests a picture of intense agricultural activity, based upon a mixed arable/pastoral economy. Evidence accumulated from the Eller Beck sites in the Lune Valley[71] suggests an extensive system of 'celtic' fields, spreading up the valley slopes and perhaps centred on the valley floor. The presence of 'mixed-farming' sites on the fells (for example, Waitby, Crosby Ravensworth and Crosby Garrett) perhaps indicates an attempt to utilise the slopes in a manner similar to that of the valleys themselves with cultivation carried probably to a higher altitude than nowadays.[72] On the whole, however, the higher-level sites (that is, above approximately 800 feet) carry, in the evidence of dykes and large 'fields', the indications of stock-management and pastoralism.[73] In the case of Eller Beck and Waitby, it has been shown that in the later Roman period there is evidence of arable land giving way to a pastoral use.[74] Such distinctions will obviously have been influenced by local environmental circumstances and by changing economic conditions.

As we have seen, rural settlement is identified in generally separate (if not isolated)

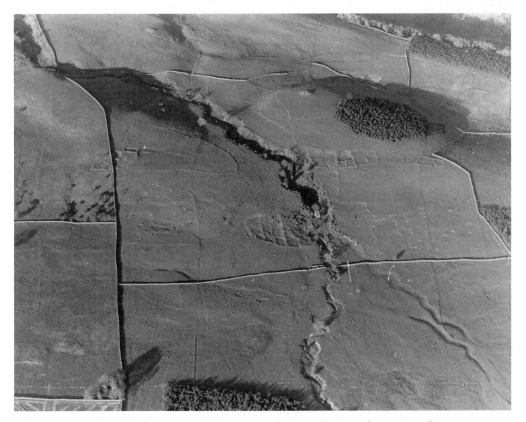

Plate 72. Eller Beck: Romano-British agricultural landscape. (*Photograph courtesy of Manunair*)

Plate 73. Collingholme: Romano-British farm. (*Photograph courtesy of Lancaster University Archaeological Unit*)

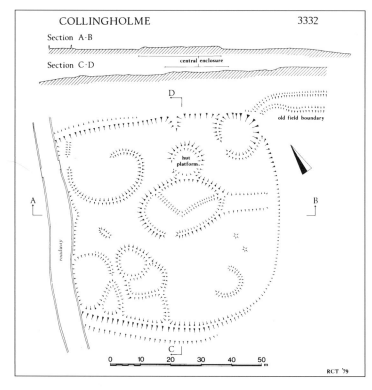

COLLINGHOLME   3332

Section A-B

Section C-D
                                        central enclosure

D

                                                          old field boundary

                                    hut
                                    platform

A   B

roadway

C

0   10   20   30   40   50
                                          m

RCT '79

Figure 8. Collingholme: Romano-British rural site.

farms – either rectilinear (as at Cantsfield near the confluence of the Lune and the Greta) or curvilinear (as at Wolsty Hall on the Solway Plain).[75] Most appear to be best described as single farmsteads rather than grouped as 'villages',[76] and generally display single entrances. Rectilinear and curvilinear forms appear to exist contemporaneously, although the rectilinear forms may be more commonly associated with field-systems. They are generally wholly enclosed, presumably to exclude marauders – human or animal – although some, as at Crosby Ravensworth, are partly unenclosed.

Whilst finds of artefacts (in addition to typological analysis) will permit relatively easy recognition of sites which belong to the Romano-British period, the paucity of these artefacts usually precludes close dating. It is generally held that the more settled conditions which prevailed from the late-second/early-third centuries provided a major stimulus to settlement expansion, although some sites are undoubtedly earlier than this. Expansion includes not just the appearance of new sites, but also the development of existing ones, as happened at Cross Hill[77] (Penrith), where a circular house gave way to rectangular buildings; such a development could suggest the influence of the *vicus* building-types, and thus carry chronological and cultural implications. Care needs, however, to be taken as change over a long period may be involved; for example, at Gauber High Pasture (in Upper Ribblesdale),[78] excavation demonstrated that a rectilinear building on a Romano-British site was in fact of ninth-century date. Conversely, excavations at Fingland showed clear evidence of a circular structure associated with late Roman pottery.[79] Whilst the huts might be placed anywhere within the enclosures, a striking phenomemon is found at Castle Folds on Orton Scar,[80] where a defensive stone wall circuit has circular and rectilinear buildings constructed against its interior face.

The usage of rural sites has again to be generally inferred from the few examples which have been the subject of study. It is self-evident that economic advantage will have lain behind a great deal that was done; the realisation of such advantage might range from the position of a farm close to the Romano-British communications and site network to the co-operative management of land which may be visible in the larger field systems. The positioning of many sites tends to indicate that they were intended to take advantage of lower land for arable purposes and higher land for stock management. Such arable usage would presumably include the growing of crops for sale and for winter feed for the stock. The smaller fields intended for arable usage were probably demarcated with low stone banks, whilst larger fields associated with higher turf banks were presumably intended for stock management.

We can, therefore, see that in general cereal and hay cultivation took place in ploughed land in the valleys and the lower slopes, whilst grazing for animals was provided on the higher slopes, presumably utilising different areas according to season. It should also be noticed that land-use was not necessarily static; the Eller Beck complex has shown arable land given over to pastoral use in the later Roman period. Some field systems, however, may always have been intended for pastoralist use, as at Aughertree Fell on the northern slopes of the Lake District, or at Stone Carr (Penrith) where fields were bounded by deep ditches. Whilst much of the pastoralism was concerned with cattle and the many uses to which they could be put, we should not forget the role of sheep beyond the provision of food. Finds of textiles at Vindolanda demonstrate the potential significance of sheep farming and the local processing of the wool. There is no reason to suppose that this may not have been carried out by local farmers, producing amongst other things the rather shapeless garments in which the 'cloaked deities' from Housesteads are depicted – possibly the *birrus britannicus* of Diocletian's Price Edict.

Whilst crop-growing and stock-management provided a living for a large section of the rural community, it should be noticed that for some hunting must have remained more of a living than a pastime. Areas of woodland will have provided a habitat for red deer and wild boar, which could clearly have made an economic contribution.

In short, whilst it has to be said that our knowledge is very selective, it is becoming possible to see a degee of integration between Roman and native in the north-west, which exists on the economic, social and religious levels.[81] The evidence will be seen principally within the urban context, and in the rural environment in the close vicinity of fort/*vicus* sites. The wider rural community will have generated what was required in taxation, and in some cases, a surplus for sale. However, that the volume of that surplus never reached major proportions in the north-west is clear from the general inability of the *vici* to prosper without active support from a military presence. In this sense, Romanisation in the north-west may have advanced – no doubt more for some than others – but it did not attain the level of urbanisation and wealth-creation that we see further south.

Clearly, there is much research to be done,

particularly on the detailed nature of the economic basis of the sites. Whilst aerial survey and field-work will continue to advance the picture, the excavation of more sites is clearly required. It is however possible with the present state of the evidence to see in part the relationship between the Roman troops and the native population – whether as craftsmen or farmers. To a degree, all were harmonised into a Romano-British economy; the native population was producing goods, manufactured or agricultural, on a commercial as well as a taxation basis, for this will explain the presence of items like Samian pottery on native sites, which must have been acquired in return for goods.

In short, therefore, it would appear to be far from the truth to argue for a 'conquerors and vanquished' type of relationship in the north-west. The Romans were a stimulus; within limits the local population became Romanised. Whilst progress was less marked and dramatic than in lowland Britain, it would still be reasonable to assert that Roman and native lived together to mutual advantage, and that north-west England enjoyed and benefited from the *Pax Romana*.

Footnotes

1. Strabo *Geographia* IV. 5.2.
2. Millet, 1990; Whittaker, 1994.
3. *Life of Agricola* 30, 5.
4. For all questions relating to the Roman army, see Webster, 1970.
5. *RIB* 601; Shotter, 1973b.
6. Dio Cassius, *History of Rome* LXXII. 16.
7. *RIB* 600.
8. Rivet, 1970.
9. Ward, 1973; Hassall, 1976.
10. Richmond and Crawford, 1949.
11. E.g. Richardson G. G. S. and Richardson A., 1980.
12. See my discussions in Potter, 1979 and Jones and Shotter, 1988.
13. Hassall, 1976; cf. Richmond, 1935 and Heurgon, 1951.
14. See above on p. 57.

15. E.g. the bath-house and basilica at Lancaster (*RIB* 605) which were rebuilt in the 260s.
16. *RIB* 933.
17. *JRS* LV (1965), 224; the inscription is of mid-third century date.
18. *Britannia* XII (1981), 325f and XIII (1982), 343f.
19. McCarthy, 1990.
20. Birley E. B., 1953; Potter, 1979, 195 (the milestone is recorded as *RIB* 2283). The possibility of other *civitates* in the north is explored by Jones R. F. J., 1981, who mentions Kirkby Thore as a possible centre.
21. Higham and Jones, 1985.
22. Shotter, 1990 and 1995b.
23. *Britannia* XVI (1985), 276.
24. Shotter, 1995a.
25. Salway (1980) suggests the possible sharing of responsibility between the fort-commander

and the nearest civilian authority – a suggestion based upon the Roman jurist, Ulpian (*Digest* 50.1, 30)

26. *RIB* 1700 (cf. *RIB* 899 from Old Carlisle).
27. Richmond and Steer, 1957.
28. The name is given in the Ravenna Cosmography as BRESNETENACI VETERANORUM; for a discussion see Richmond, 1945.
29. Potter, 1979, 187 (Watercrook).
30. See Smith (1959), for the Palmyrene sculptor at South Shields; cf. *RIB* 864 from Maryport for a man from Galatia in Asia Minor.
31. Tylecote, 1962, 222ff.
32. Jones G. D. B., 1974.
33. McCarthy, 1986.
34. Jones G. D. B., 1975.
35. Birley R. E., 1977.
36. See Jones and Shotter, 1988, 61ff; Shotter and White, 1990, 23; *RIB* 602 gives details about the officer concerned. *Note*: The '*mansio*' at Vindolanda has now been re-interpreted as part of the *principia* (headquarters) of the Severan fort.
37. *Britannia* X (1979), 353.
38. *RIB* 955 (Carlisle) and 787 (Brougham).
39. *RIB* 856.
40. Penney and Shotter, 1996.
41. Potter, 1979, 79ff.
42. Thompson, 1976.
43. Thompson, 1965, 84.
44. Edwards, 1971.
45. Grimes, 1930; Thompson, 1965, 53ff.
46. *Britannia* XIII (1982), 352.
47. Bellhouse, 1960b.
48. Hogg, 1965.
49. Leather and Webster, 1988.
50. Shotter, 1983.
51. Thompson, 1965, 60ff.
52. Jones G. D. B., 1974, 147f.
53. Thompson, 1965, 67ff; Hinchliffe and Williams, 1992.
54. Hartley and Webster, 1973.
55. Strickland, 1995, 12.
56. Webster, 1975.
57. *Britannia* XV (1984), 286.
58. King, 1970.
59. Branigan, 1980.
60. For Kirk Sink, see *Britannia* V (1974), 416 and VI (1975), 238; for Eaton-by-Tarporley, see *Britannia* XIII (1982), 353.
61. King, 1978.
62. E.g. Richardson A., (1982), for the discussion of an area near Old Penrith.
63. See now the distribution-map in Higham, 1980, 42.
64. Bowman and Thomas, 1983.
65. Higham and Jones, 1975; see also Haselgrove in Newman, 1997.
66. Jones G. D. B., 1979, 79ff; for a site at Salford, see *Britannia* XX (1989), 281.
67. *YAJ* XLI (1966), 559–60; King, 1978.
68. Higham and Jones, 1975; Higham, 1978; 1979; 1980; 1982.
69. Jones G. D. B., 1975; Bowman and Thomas, 1983; Davies, 1971; Manning, 1975.
70. Richardson G. G. S., 1977, 57.
71. Lowndes, 1963 and 1964; Higham, 1979; Shotter and White, 1995, 58ff.
72. Pennington, 1970.
73. E.g. Aughertree Fell (Bellhouse, 1967).
74. Higham and Jones, 1975, 40ff; Higham, 1979, 34.
75. Blake, 1959, 7ff.
76. Higham, 1980, 41.
77. *Britannia* VIII (1977), 377.
78. King, 1978.
79. Richardson G. G. S., 1977.
80. Richmond, 1933; Higham, 1979.
81. Manning, 1975.

7. The Later Years

We have seen that Severus by armed force and then his son, Caracalla, by diplomacy appear to have secured with the Scottish tribes some kind of agreement which apparently brought a large measure of peace to the north for a good deal of the third century. It is less clear, however, how far the military grip was relaxed: a major problem in the approach to this question lies in the nature of the evidence: in general, the pottery is less clearly dated for the third and fourth centuries than it is for the first and second. Further, coin-loss evidence is also less reliable for the period, being complicated by the monetary crises that deepened as the third century wore on, and by the *annona militaris* – the practice of paying troops at least partly in kind, which started late in the century.

It is certain that (with the exception of the forts) the Cumberland coast defences, which had been abandoned late in the second century, were not generally in use during the third – although, as we shall see, there is evidence which suggests a selective reactivation in the fourth. Building-inscriptions and other evidence of building activity indicate that some forts were certainly being kept in repair in the first half of the third century (for example, at Ribchester, Manchester, Lancaster, Watercrook, Old Carlisle, Old Penrith.) [1] The second half of the century, however, presents a more confused picture.

In the first place, the civilian authority that was in being by the 260s in the form of the *civitas Carvetiorum* implies internal peace in the north-west and perhaps a desire to place more of the burden of administration on to the local population. It is likely, too, that Hadrian's Wall, which had seen a good deal of reconstruction and refurbishment in the late second and early third centuries, was left free from enemy-attack during this period: the result was probably that garrisons were reduced or even removed, as certainly happened at Watercrook, where a fresh coin of A.D. 320 in the top of the ditch-fill implies demilitarisation by that stage. There is evidence to suggest that some Hadrian's Wall forts (for example, Castlesteads, Birdoswald, Halton Chesters, Rudchester and Wallsend) and the wall itself fell into a state of considerable disrepair. It is possible that these sites were not actually abandoned, but held by token numbers: it has been suggested that the new, smaller type of barrack-block shown to have been built at Housesteads, Birdoswald and other wall forts in the early fourth century implies a reduced and perhaps less well organised garrison, or perhaps a population of both military personnel and civilians.

Secondly, changes in the nature of the army command structure, where unit commanders were much more likely to have been soldiers who had risen from the ranks than the men of higher social status that had been usual before, may have meant a loss of discipline. Further, fewer of the troops were now formed into regular auxiliary units, and more reliance was placed on the units of irregulars. Internally, therefore, peaceful conditions together with the contemporary state of the army itself seem to have combined to produce a relaxed, if not lax, holding of the north-west in the later third century.

If the province was not troubled with anxieties on its northern frontier, there were certainly problems elsewhere, which will have had their effects in the north. Inflation ran wild in the middle of the third century – at least partly due to the fact that successive emperors in their efforts to maintain their positions 'printed money' in order to hand out bribes – that is, funds they did not possess. The resultant chaos is evidenced by the large number of 'radiate copies', often of very poor standard, which were in circulation; there were clearly a number of copying centres for these in the north including (probably) Brougham and Carlisle. Further, attempts made by emperors between c. A.D. 270 and 300 to remove this 'bad money' seem in the case of Britain to have largely failed. The demoralising effect of economic chaos can be paralleled from more recent history.

Again, Severus' reforms of the army and its command structure, which led to promotion through the ranks to senior army command – and higher – had the effect by the middle of the century of making anarchy virtually endemic in the empire. It led not only to a constant stream of 'pretenders', but eventually to breakaway movements such as the independent Empire of the Gauls (*Imperium Galliarum*) in which between A.D. 259 and 273 the Germanies, Gaul and Britain completely severed their connection with the central government and its officials. How far (if at all) this led to the removal of troops from Britain is unclear. The British army's loyalty to the new rulers is evidenced by such inscriptions as that commemorating the rebuilding of the Lancaster bathhouse,[2] from

which the name of Postumus, the creator of the *Imperium Galliarum*, was subsequently removed (that is, after A.D. 273).

Although this rebellion collapsed in A.D. 273, to be followed by a series of rather stronger central government emperors, the eventual 'solution', enacted by Diocletian, was the establishment of first a dyarchy, and a little later, a tetrarchy which consisted of two senior figures (*Augusti*) and two junior (*Caesares*), each of whom was responsible for a section of imperial territory. However, in Britain, Carausius, who had been appointed by Maximian (Diocletian's fellow-Augustus), to keep the English Channel and the North Sea free of pirates, decided that the principle of split power could be extended: he minted a coin with three obverse heads (his own, Diocletian's and Maximian's)with the legend CARAVSIVS ET FRATRES SVI ('Carausius and his brothers'). Since Diocletian and Maximian failed to regard Carausius as their brother, his position in A.D. 287 became *ipso facto* rebellious. Carausius maintained himself until A.D. 293, when he was murdered

Plate 74. Brougham: Late-third century coin-hoard. The coin in the centre is a 'legitimate' *antoninianus* of the Emperor, Valerian, whilst the coins in the top and bottom rows are locally-made 'radiate copies'. (*Carlisle Museum and Art Gallery*)

by his associate, Allectus, who survived until ousted three years later by the central government in the person of Constantius Chlorus, who was 'Caesar' in the west.

The details of the rebellion do not concern us except in so far as it was a period when attention was paid to the problems of coastal defence. Although not of uniform date, the Saxon-Shore fort system in the south-east owed a good deal of its impetus to this period, and Allectus' 'Galley' coin-reverses stress a similar preoccupation. The new forts were architecturally very different from their predecessors, particularly with their artillery bastions, and indicate a transition in Roman tactical thinking from the 'police-station' to the 'defended strong-point'.

The effect of Allectus' attempts to hold his rebel island against the tetrarchs has long been thought to have been a denuding of northern garrisons, leading to an attack on the frontier from the north. There is evidence for both delapidation and demolition in the north in the late third century, and for fire damage at Ravenglass. An inscription records Constantius' involvement in rebuilding at Birdoswald, and other forts of Hadrian's Wall and the hinterland certainly saw reconstruction in the early fourth century.[3] But no evidence points unequivocally to coherent enemy attack at that time.

Constantius was in Britain on at least two occasions – in 296 to crush the rebellion of Carausius and Allectus, and again campaigning in the north in 305–6 against the Picts, and it may well have been in the course of this second visit that he set in train the rebuilding programme of forts in the north – not only on Hadrian's Wall, but also at sites like Bainbridge and other Pennine forts. Recent work at Housesteads has demonstrated that the third-century barrack-block in the fort's north-east corner had probably decayed, and was replaced early in the fourth century by a far less formal unit consisting of 'chalets' of variable size which were probably stone-built only to half-height. There is similar evidence at Birdoswald of 'chalet-style' buildings replacing earlier barracks; and a contemporary aisled building may be a *basilica equestris exercitatoria* (cavalry drill-hall) attached to the Headquarters.[4] The new type

Plate 75. Housesteads: 'Chalet'-barracks.

of barracks is presumably to be taken as indicating a different type of usage from that for which the building's predecessor was intended – either a combined military and civilian purpose, or army units of a different type, although this is left in doubt by the 'wall sub-section' in the *Notitia* and difficulties surrounding its date of reference (third or fourth century); the sub-section lists the Wall-forts as garrisoned by the same units as are known from third-century inscriptions, which has led to the suggestion[5] that the chronological reference of this section may in fact be third and not fourth century.

It may be that Constantius' view of and presence in Britain brought about a radical 're-think' of tactics to face the new enemy – the Picts; the post of *Dux Britanniarum* (the northern military commander) was probably created at this time. Further, the rebuilding noted at hinterland-forts may suggest that the notion of 'defence in depth' was coming to supersede the idea of the wall as a 'curtain-barrier'. Indeed, the wall itself, as distinct from its forts, may have been less important in the fourth-century arrangements.[6] Thus the post of *Dux Britanniarum* was now added to that of *Comes Litoris Saxonici*, and the pair led the two fourth-century 'frontier' armies in Britain: these armies were distinct from the 'field army' which the emperors took on campaign with them. In A.D. 315, Constantine took the title of *Britannicus Maximus*; a particular point of reference is not known, though it may have had some relation to the west coast,[7] or possibly to a continued attention to in-depth readiness, for which Constantine was in fact criticised in antiquity.[8] Possibly we should date the establishment of the west-coast 'Saxon-shore' forts to this period, although reliable dates are not to hand for Cardiff, Caernarvon or Caer Gybi, and the new fort at Lancaster would appear to be a decade or so later than this.

It is difficult to say how far (if at all) a coherent west-coast defence system existed. That the Bristol Channel was a significant base at least later in the century seems to be suggested by the letters PR REL, (interpreted as *Praefectus reliquationis classis*) found on a mosaic in the Nodons temple at Lydney. This, together with the forts at Cardiff, Caernarvon and Caer Gybi, stresses the importance and vulnerabilty of the Welsh coasts; it is further likely that a fleet base in the Bristol Channel will have rendered redundant the legionary fortress at Caerleon (which does not appear to have outlasted the third century). The Bristol Channel base will have linked to the still maintained legionary fortress at Chester, on the Dee estuary, and thence to Lancaster on the Lune estuary, where probably about A.D. 330–340 an approximately nine-acre enclosure with polygonal corner bastions was built on a different alignment from earlier forts. Excavations[9] have also suggested the abandonment of *vicus*-buildings in Lancaster at about this time. It may be significant that Cockersands Moss, just south of Lancaster, was the find-spot of two statuettes of Nodons[10] (now lost), thus providing a possible link with Lydney and the Bristol Channel.

In what must have been an increasingly unstable situation, it is unclear how long life could have been maintained at a reasonable standard in the largely undefended *vici*. Obviously, the length of life of a *vicus* will have represented a response to local conditions, and there is no general date in the north-west that can be applied to the closure of *vici*. At Ribchester, for example, changing environmental conditions may have forced the closure of parts of the *vicus* as early as the later second century. Recent excavations at Lancaster have suggested that *vicus*-buildings may have been in the process of abandonment towards the middle of the fourth century, and this may have coincided with the building of the new 'Saxon-shore' type of fort on Castle Hill, which is dated to *c.* A.D. 330–340. Although the interior structures of most forts in the fourth century are ill-known, it may well be, as we have seen, that what is known would have been consistent with occupation by a population made up of soldiers and

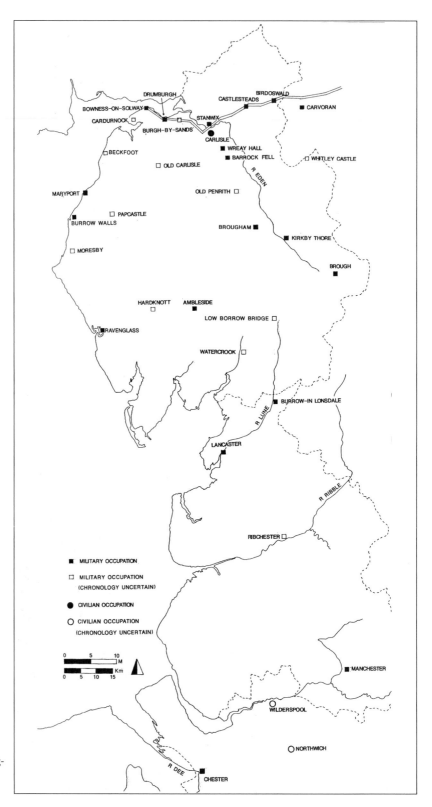

Figure 9.
Roman sites in
North-West Eng-
land occupied
after A.D. 367.

Plate 76. Lancaster: The 'Wery Wall' (arrowed); in the foreground are the remains of a bath-house over which it was built.

Plate 77. Caer Gybi: Fourth-century fort wall, with bastions.

civilians. In this case, the forts would have been becoming more akin to 'fortified villages'.

We may assume that in a fast-changing situation, flexibility was a key word: Vegetius describes camouflaged scout-ships (*pictae*) which were used in the fourth century; Lancaster and Morecambe Bay may have seen novel use made of the soldiers of a *Numerus Barcariorum*,[11] whose normal function will have been lighterage.

Arrangements further north on the coast

are not easy to describe precisely: the coastal forts of Ravenglass, Moresby, Maryport and Beckfoot were all occupied in the fourth century, although in the cases of Moresby and Beckfoot it is not clear how long that occupation was sustained. Burrow Walls[12] has produced little other than fourth-century pottery, and may well have been a new – or at least very substantially remodelled – fort of the period. There appears also to have been fourth-century reoccupation of some of the long-abandoned sites of the coastal system; at Cardurnock (MF 5),[13] for example, pottery suggested occupation both before and after A.D. 367, although the absence of such material at Biglands House (MF1) and Swarthy Hill (MF 21) is sufficient to warn us that this was not a full-scale recommissioning.

The context for some of this work may well have been the visit to Britain in the winter of A.D. 342–3 of the emperor, Constans. The mere fact that the visit was made in the winter is sufficient to indicate that it must have been connected with some emergency, and not just routine in nature. It is known that Constans' visit was in part at least concerned with the *areani* or undercover agents; trouble with them certainly implies disturbance on the northern frontier.

The state of Britain at this time clearly should not be divorced from imperial politics: Constantine's death in 337 had left the Roman world divided between his three surviving sons, Constantine II, Constans and Constantius II. Britain had come within the responsibility of Constantine II, but he was killed in Italy in conflict with Constans in 340. Problems arising out of possible troop withdrawals from Britain by Constantine II and out of possible disaffection in Britain following upon Constantine II's death may have left a situation uncertain enough to encourage Britain's enemies to take advantage – which may well have been the situation with which Constans intended to deal.

The death of Constans in 350 at the hands of a group who proclaimed Magnentius as his successor also suggests a continuing disturbance in Britain: for evidence such as the frequency of his coins suggests that

Plate 78. Birdoswald: Blocked eastern gateway.

Plate 79. Late Roman gold coins: Theodosius (*left*) from Muncaster Castle; Valentinian II (*right*) from Carlisle. (*The photograph of the coin of Valentinian II is reproduced by courtesy of Carlisle Archaeological Unit*)

Magnentius had particular strength in Britain. It is also likely that he again weakened the provinces' military potential by taking troops to Europe to assert his cause. Magnentius' final defeat at the hands of Constantius II in 353 will have brought still further demoralisation to Britain in its wake – first, two further defeats to add to that in which Constantine II had been killed, and second, a witch-hunt in the province following upon Constantius' reassertion of authority.[14]

In 355 Constantius appointed as western *Caesar* his cousin Julian. Although Julian's period showed in a sense the strength of Britain in that in 359 it was possible to use the province as a supply base for his efforts to re-establish the Rhine frontier, yet less than two years later the continuing insecurity manifested itself in trouble with the Picts and Scotti (from Ireland),which necessitated the posting to Britain of Lupicinus, a very senior officer, with crack units of the 'field army'. The situation remained tense until it came to a head with the 'Barbarian Conspiracy'[15] in 367, in which all of the enemies of Roman Britain appear to have attacked at once. Such an apparently unlikely event as a 'conspiracy' is made perhaps less unlikely when it is real-

ised how deep was the involvement of Romanised 'barbarians' in Roman political and military affairs. It is possible that leaked information about the contemporary difficulties of the emperor Valentinian I was the trigger for this action:[16] the opportunity was evidently enhanced by the treacherous activities of the *areani*[17] who were disbanded in the wake of the catastrophe, together with the 'outpost-forts' on the western end of the frontier.

Valentinian's response was to send to Britain, again with a crack 'field army', Theodosius, the father of the later emperor, Theodosius. Ammianus makes it clear that the situation – military, urban and rural – was one of almost total disarray. We should, however, beware of assuming that every archaeological sign of trouble relates to this particular year: as we have seen, 367 had been the climax of nearly two-and-a-half decades of uncertainty and raiding. Theodosius' achievement was considerable – restabilisation of the military situation, the rebuilding of forts and towns, and the restoration of rural peace.

That the majority of north-western sites either survived the barbarian attack or were rebuilt and occupied after, is clear from the ubiquity of the calcite-gritted wares that were the characteristic product of the Crambeck potteries of east Yorkshire in the second half of the fourth century. Similarly, the absence of this type of pottery provides a good indicator of forts that were probably not included in the restoration. It would certainly appear that there was no attempt to recover forts to the north of Hadrian's Wall, and doubt hangs over the continued use of some forts to the south of it (for example, Ribchester and Watercrook), though it has to be stressed in the consideration of this question, as with others, that a number of the forts have as yet no evidence upon which a statement about their occupation at this stage could be based.

Forts in the north-west which were reconstructed in this period show no sign of the 'Saxon-shore' architecture that had been employed in Wales and at Lancaster earlier in the century. However, one feature of the rebuilding may have been 'learned' from the 'Saxon-shore' forts – the blocking or narrowing of gateways, which has been recognised at a number of northern forts, and most recently at Birdoswald on Hadrian's Wall. At that site, the north carriageway of the east gate and the south carriageway of the west gate were both closed, presumably in an effort to achieve the impenetrability which was a feature of the 'Saxon-shore' forts. At both Ravenglass and Bowness-on-Solway[18] excavation has shown that a new constructional technique for internal buildings was employed in this final phase. Instead of foundation beams, buildings were apparently supported on a 'frame' of heavily-packed posts.

Reconstruction is everywhere to be seen in the forts of the Wall and its hinterland; for example, the granaries at Birdoswald were remodelled,[19] and the fact that the sub-floor space was in-filled suggests that the reconstructed buildings carried a different purpose from the originals. In addition, a hall-like building was built partly over a previous granary; this was supported on timber posts set on to pads. Work extended also to new sites;

Plate 80. Birdoswald: Timber-built 'hall', constructed over the north granary of the fort.

for example, two new fortlets are known to have guarded the road south from Carlisle – at Wreay Hall and Barrock Fell.[20] Nothing, however, is as yet known of the internal layout of these sites. Recent research has shown the possibility of another such site at Cummersdale.

The coasts, too, received attention as they had obviously demonstrated their vulnerability. As noted above, building-work belonging to the second half of the fourth century has been recognised at most coastal forts in the north-west; and there is evidence to suggest that some parts of the second-century system between Bowness-on-Solway and Maryport were brought back into use. Finds of late fourth century coins in and around Barrow-in-Furness[21] and of a gold *solidus* of Theodosius at Muncaster Castle suggest the possibility of sites in those areas too – possibly in the form of coastal towers. In addition, the east coast of northern England was given a new series of strongly-built signal-towers. In all, then, Theodosius' reconstruction work in the north was a strikingly thorough attempt to take account of all of the problems encountered in the 'Barbarian Conspiracy'. It is probable that recognition of Theodosius' work is to be seen in the use of the title *Valentia* to apply to the whole of Britain, in honour of the ruling house of Valentinian.[22]

Although it is not clear when Britain finally lost an institutional connection with the Roman empire, it cannot have been much later than A.D. 400–420. The last decades of the fourth century, however, showed no obvious slackening in the north of building and maintenance activities, though it is not clear how far these were originated centrally or whether they were local initiatives, as Romano-British communities learned to become more self-reliant.

In 382 Magnus Maximus was sent to campaign in the north, though he was subsequently to achieve greater fame through his attempt to unite Gaul and Britain in a single command, and presumably to resuscitate ideas of the defunct *Imperium Galliarum*. He maintained himself until 388, and appears to have recorded some positive achievements in strengthening the security of the west coast, through the establishment of tribal protectorates. However, although the sources are by no means unequivocal in interpretation, it would appear that Maximus' removal of troops to Gaul once again created a volatile situation in the north; indeed it is likely that security matters in the north remained uncertain until another major outbreak, probably in 398, which brought the last positive response by Rome to British affairs. Honorius sent over the Vandal general, Stilicho, who appears to have restored order for the moment, but who either took back to Europe with him, or was closely followed by, a legion from northern Britain.[23]

For ten more years – the first decade of the fifth century – contact was maintained, though increasingly tenuously. It would appear that after about 402 no further supplies of money arrived to pay the army (or such as was left of it); further, evidence suggests an increasing independence within Britain. The second half of the decade saw a new series of 'local' emperors elevated by the army, which we may assume to be the army's response to the failing support from Rome. To this may be linked the action in 408 of independently-minded Britons, perhaps influenced by the 'independent' religious views of the Pelagian heresy, in expelling Roman officials and organising the defence of Britain themselves. This was probably not, however, a universal view, as others hoped for a renewal and strengthening of links with the rest of the empire. But the 'independents' had been wise: there was to be no more help from Rome, and Britain's formal place in the empire had now lapsed. These 'independent' actions, however, should not be taken to indicate a rejection of everything Roman. The rejection was political; the inhabitants of Britain after all, whether supporting or opposing Rome's current position, were Romano-British. As many excavations, particularly of the towns, have shown,[24] the people clearly remained for a considerable time, though perhaps in varying degrees, within the Roman cultural orbit. At Carlisle, for example, the recent discovery of a gold *solidus* of the emperor, Valentinian II (*c.* A.D. 392), stratified within a hypocaust system indicates that the building of which the hypocaust was a part must have been consciously renovated in a Roman style well into the fifth century.[25] Indeed, the survival of Roman Carlisle is in a sense attested by Bede's description of St. Cuthbert's visit.[26]

In general, however, the physical fate of north-western sites can only be guessed at, particularly since the means of dating in the fifth century are far from perfect: repairing of chronologically-late vessels, worn late fourth-century coin issues and finds of such vessels as African red-slip ware, all suggest a continued attempt to maintain the familiar way of life. Indeed Christianity, though not always a politically and militarily unifying force, will nonetheless have provided a link with Rome's cultural background. In the north-west, as elsewhere, we may reasonably imagine therefore that Roman fortifications continued to provide protection – particularly if we judge from sites like Lancaster, Brough and Brougham, where the medieval castles were erected in some kind of association with the presumably still surviving Roman wall-circuits.

Plate 81. Gauber High Pasture (Upper Ribblesdale): Viking 'long-house', constructed over a Romano-British farm. (*Photograph courtesy of Alan King*)

The length of survival of Romano-British sites in the north-west obviously varied according to local conditions. As we have seen, some *vici* may have ceased to function relatively early; the apparent demilitarisation of the fort at Watercrook in the third century seems to have brought the life of the *vicus* to an end – even though there is some evidence for renewal of military activity in the later fourth century. At Ribchester, activity in the known *vicus*-area seems to have come to an end in *c.* A.D. 200; there is no obvious explanation of this. Some sites, such as Walton-le-Dale and Wilderspool were apparently running down during the early third century, although some activity seems to have continued into the fourth. Recent excavation at Lancaster has suggested that *vicus*-activity possibly continued until the middle of the fourth century. Clearly, no single explanation will cover all of these situations.

It may well be that in the fourth century, there was a growing tendency for military and civilian personnel alike to enjoy the protection afforded by the forts, particularly remote ones, such as Low Borrow Bridge. In this regard, it is worth making the point that, in the face of troop withdrawals during the fourth century, an increasing proportion of the garrisons were probably locally recruited: it will thus have been perfectly natural for them and their families to have regarded themselves as permanently settled in their own particular areas. Recent excavations at Birdoswald, for example, have suggested, that the fort may have become more like a 'village' where a local group, perhaps with little contact with the outside world, assumed responsibility for defending and supporting itself. However, the long-term survival of such sites was unlikely; few of the north-west's fort/towns survived as going concerns even into the middle ages let alone to the present day. Long-term survival required economic strength and links with the outside world. It is not surprising therefore that the north-west's survivors are generally well positioned either on navigable waterways – Chester,

Wilderspool/Warrington, Walton-le-Dale/ Preston, Manchester, Lancaster, Carlisle, – or at crucial places on the road system, with the economic and military strength that that gave: hence the defended sites across Stainmore were as important in the middle ages as they had been in the Roman period. In other words, for survival, a site clearly needed to have a significance that transcended its mere place in the Roman defensive network.

In the country, the situation – due to even less excavation than in the towns – is less clear. We may assume that besides self-sufficiency two other factors must have been of crucial importance in determining the long-term survival of sites – the availability to inhabitants of markets to service and their ability to continue to work unmolested. The degree of fulfilment of these conditions must have been variable then, as well as unquantifiable now: we may, however, imagine that sites probably thrived and were left from time to time, but later returned to. A recent demonstration of this has been the discovery of Viking occupation on the site of Romano-British settlement at Gauber High Pasture in Upper Ribblesdale.[27] A striking view of how long-term this process might be is the recently

excavated site immediately to the south of the fort at Maiden Castle-on-Stainmore, where the latest structure on a site that showed both pre-Roman and Roman activity was a nineteenth-century cottage.

Thus, the last years of the occupation obviously show a decline in (eventually) the degree of Roman military commitment, and therefore the ability of the population to continue its established life-style. As elsewhere, the northern tribesmen must have been thrown increasingly on their own resources; indeed such elements of the Roman army that remained probably disbanded themselves, melting into the local community. Thus, they and the local tribesmen were now forced back into an economy where the major, perhaps sole, economic preoccupation was self-provision. Without the markets and the protection which the army had afforded, there was little else. Without the discipline which Rome had brought, the factional rivalry – no doubt largely over the ownership of resources which had characterised the pre-Roman period – returned to the north-west. The local tribesmen continued to cope with new problems, but the 'Roman Interlude' was essentially over.

Footnotes

1. For Hadrian's Wall, see Breeze and Dobson, 1976, 202f.
2. *RIB* 605; see Shotter and White, 1990, 60.
3. Johnson, 1980, 83ff; Wilkes, 1965.
4. For Birdoswald, see *Britannia* XXI (1990), 316.
5. Gillam, 1949.
6. Mann, 1974; Ferrill, 1991.
7. Eusebius, *Life of Constantine* I. 8 and 25.
8. Zosimus II. 34.
9. Shotter and White, 1990, 36.
10. *RIB* 616 and 617; these statuettes are now lost; Shotter, 1973b; Shotter and White, 1995, 97f.
11. *RIB* 601; Shotter, 1973b; Shotter and White, 1990, 59.
12. Bellhouse, 1955.
13. Simpson and Hodgson, 1947; Bellhouse, 1989, 18ff.
14. Ammianus Marcellinus XIV. 5, 6–9; Hind, 1983, 1ff.

15. The term applied to it by Ammianus (XXVII. 8).
16. Salway, 1981, 374f.
17. Ammianus XXVII. 3,8; Shotter, 1996, 121; Gillam, Jobey and Welsby, 1993; Austen, 1990.
18. Potter, 1979.
19. See *Britannia* XIX (1988), 436.
20. Wreay Hall (Bellhouse, 1953); Barrock Fell (Collingwood, 1931). Recent excavations (1996) have shown the possibility of another at Cummersdale.
21. Shotter, 1989, 43; Shotter, 1990, 239ff.
22. Johnson, 1980, 98.
23. Johnson, 1980, 103; Miller, 1975.
24. E.g. Barker, 1975.
25. See *Britannia* XX (1989), 254f.
26. Bede, *Life of St Cuthbert*, 27.
27. King, 1978.

Conclusions

Over the years, a tolerably clear picture has developed of the effects of the Roman occupation of north-west England. However, there is scope for new enquiry, and although the body of knowledge has grown since the publication of the first edition of this book, the questions which await answers remain substantially the same.

The military aspects of occupation – forts and roads – have continued to receive a good deal of attention; the fact that new forts are still located indicates that we should remain open-minded with regard to the topographical layout of the network of occupation. In particular, although some 'chinks' of light have shone, we still await a major breakthrough in the picture of occupation in southern Cumbria. A larger lacuna is the detailed chronology of occupation of military sites; very few have as yet anything more than a very basic chronological framework, and in particular we still seek to clarify by the discovery of new sites or the further treatment of evidence from existing sites the strategy and chronology of conquest. The pattern of military dispositions still requires much investigation and fresh information – in the form of writing-tablets from waterlogged deposits, and new evidence highlighted by professional and amateur fieldworkers.

Work has continued to elucidate chronological and topographical factors concerning the occupation of the coastline of north-west England, although we still require more information on the flexibility of treatment, and in particular, how much use may have been made of the sites in the more troubled times of the fourth century.

The *vici*, too, leave many unanswered questions; in particular we have no satisfactory explanation as to why a considerable number of them seem not to have outlasted the mid-third century. Were there local conditions which were responsible, or was a more general factor at play? As yet we do not have, except on aerial photographs, anything like the full plan of a *vicus* in the north-west. This not only denies us a full picture of all the buildings that these small towns might support, but also a reasonable idea of the make-up of the populations. The organisation of the *vici* also requires further research.

In the countryside, the need is for excavation to answer some of the basic problems about development, chronology and economy; besides this the question of the economic relationship between the farms and the Roman sites needs further exploration; so too does the way in which land was allocated, and the nature of the relationship between the ex-soldiers given land at the time of their discharge and the native farmers who were the descendants of those whom the army had originally conquered. In this connection it should be remembered that large areas of the north-west have not been subjected to detailed field-work and have not as yet been covered by aerial reconnaissance.

This indicates where progress has been made and a few of the problems still requiring attention. In outline we have a fair picture of the development of the north-west in the period of Roman occupation. Studies of the immediately post-Roman period and of the so-called 'Dark Ages' may well help to illuminate the question of whether Roman influence went deep or whether it was a passing phase, though it has to be admitted that Christianity in the celtic west must have done a good deal to preserve a Roman tradition.

In conclusion, however, we now know enough to lay aside the older notions of an iron-fisted conqueror controlling a people generally hostile or sullenly passive. Rather, *Dea Brigantia* presided over territory that was in its way as Romanised as many other parts of the Empire.

Appendix I

The Brigantes, Venutius and Cartimandua

The two fullest accounts of the Brigantes to have survived in classical writers are those of the historian, Cornelius Tacitus, in *Histories* III. 45 and *Annals* XII. 40. Some of the problems inherent in the passages have been discussed in the main body of the text (see above in Chapter 3).

The passage from the *Annals*, although written later (*c.*A.D. 115) describes the earlier of the two situations – that is, in the 50s and 60s. The passage from the *Histories* (written *c.*A.D. 102) covers events leading up to Roman intervention in the 70s. Whilst there are shades of difference between the two accounts, both stress that at least some of the squabbling between Venutius and Cartimandua remained internal to the Brigantes, although the former was able to call on help from outside – perhaps from north Wales. It is also tolerably clear that the overall effect of the tensions was actually to maintain the *status quo*. The fact that Tacitus compares Venutius and Caratacus as warriors is itself of interest, and would certainly help to explain how the Brigantes were so formidable under him (that is, during Cerialis' governorship), and so much easier when he had been removed (that is, when Agricola went through the area in a single season).

I: *Annals* XII. 40

'Following the Roman capture of Caratacus, the foremost military thinker left in Britain was Venutius who, as I have already recorded,* was a Brigantian. Whilst he was married to queen Cartimandua, he enjoyed Roman protection and was a loyal ally; however, after they split up he attacked her and even became embroiled in hostilities against us. At first, the Brigantian leaders confined themselves to fighting each other, as Cartimandua cleverly trapped Venutius' brother

and dependents. Before long, however, Cartimandua's enemies became angry at the disgrace which they perceived to be involved in being ruled by a woman, and they attacked her kingdom with a hand-picked band of strong, young, warriors. We were ready for this, and made a pre-emptive strike with a force of auxiliaries which we sent in to support Cartimandua. Although these support-troops achieved little to start with, they were eventually successful; a similar reward attended the efforts of the legion which was commanded by Caesius Nasica. Didius Gallus (i.e. the provincial governor), an elderly man who was by now resting on his laurels, was happy to keep the enemy at arm's length through the actions of his subordinates.'

---

* This is a reference evidently to an earlier mention of Venutius in a portion of the *Annals* which is now lost (presumably in books VII–X, which dealt with the reign of Gaius Caligula and Claudius' early years).

II: *Histories* III.45

'The persistent rumours of civil war encouraged British morale and Venutius capitalised upon this. He was a man with a naturally violent disposition who hated everything to do with Rome. At this time, his temper was made worse as a result of a bitter personal feud with queen Cartimandua. Her influence lay in the nobility of her birth, and she had ruled over the Brigantes for some time; her power had increased as the result of her treacherous capture of king Caratacus which, it was generally thought, was the crowning glory of the emperor Claudius' British triumph. So she became wealthy, and enjoyed the luxurious lifestyle associated with success. She tired of her husband, Venutius, and gave herself instead to Vellocatus, her husband's armour-bearer, and shared her kingdom with him. The immediate effect of this was a shock-wave which ran throughout the royal family.

'The Brigantian tribesmen retained their loyalty to Venutius, although the new husband prospered as a result of the queen's infatuation with him and the harsh control which she exercised over her people. So Venutius called up help from outside, and this prompted the Brigantes to defect from Cartimandua who was left in real danger of defeat. So she appealed for Roman assistance; in the event, our auxiliary cavalry and infantry units, after an uphill struggle, rescued the queen from her immediate peril. As a result, Venutius was left in control of the kingdom, whilst we had a full-scale war on our hands.' The problems of relating these passages are considerable largely because of the vagueness of Tacitus' chronology; the only events which can be dated are the capture of Caratacus (A.D. 51) and the Roman civil war (A.D. 68–69). For discussions, see Hanson and Campbell, 1986, Braund, 1984, Shotter, 1995a. The suggestion that the enigmatic 'elliptical building' in the fortress at Chester was put at the ousted queen's disposal is unlikely in view of the unsuitable nature of the building.

Similarly vague in chronology and topography is Tacitus' account of Agricola's second campaign in which he appears formally to have added the Brigantes to the province.

III: *Life of Agricola* 20

'In early summer, Agricola prepared his army for the year's campaigning season. He was himself much in evidence on the march, praising those who were well- disciplined and chivvying the stragglers. Agricola chose the camp-sites himself and personally reconnoitred estuaries and woods. In all of this, the enemy was given little respite from the sudden raids which the Romans launched on them. When he had made sufficient use of such intimidatory tactics, he would take the heat off and show them the attraction of peace. As a result, many groups, which had up to that time lived independently, gave hostages, laid aside their hostility and accepted being fenced in with forts and garrisons. This was all done with such attention to detail that no new area had ever become part of the province with as little trouble as this.'

Appendix II:
Known Dispositions of Roman Units in North-West England

Chester	Leg II Adiutrix
	Leg XX Valeria Victrix (inscriptions give dates from mid-second to mid-third century)
Manchester	Vex of Leg II and III Italica (late second century)
	Coh I Frisiavonum
	Coh III Bracaraugustanorum (possibly second century)
Castleshaw	Coh III Bracaraugustanorum
Ribchester	Ala II Asturum
	Numerus Equitum (later Ala) Sarmatarum (third century)
Lancaster	Ala Augusta
	Ala Sebosiana (mid-third century)
	Numerus Barcariorum
Bainbridge	Coh VI Nerviorum (early-third century)
Bowes	Coh IIII Breucorum (130s)
	Coh I Thracum (late-second to mid-third century)
Kirkby Thore	Ala
	Numerus militum Syrorum Sagittariorum
	Coh? Gallorum
	Coh I Vangionum (?)
	Cuneus Frisionum Germanorum
	Numerus Equitum Stratonicianorum
Hardknott	Coh IIII Delmatorum (Hadrianic)
Ravenglass	Coh I Aelia Classica
Moresby	Coh II Thracum
	Coh II Lingonum
Maryport	Coh I Hispanorum Equitata (Hadrianic)
	Coh I Delmatarum (Antonine)
	Coh I Baetasiorum
Beckfoot	Coh II Pannoniorum
Papcastle	Cuneus Frisionum Aballavensium (mid-third century)
Old Carlisle	Ala Augusta (late second to mid-third century)
Old Penrith	Coh II Gallorum Equitata (mid-third century)
	Vex Marsacarum (mid-third century)
	Vex Germanorum (mid-third century)
Stanwix	Ala Augusta Petriana milliaria torquata (late second century)
Carlisle	All British legions are recorded (II Augusta, VI Victrix, IX Hispana, XX Valeria Victrix)
Netherby	Coh I Nervana
	Coh I Aelia Hispanorum milliaria equitata (early to mid-third century)
Bewcastle	Coh I Dacorum

Vindolanda	Coh I Tungrorum
	Coh VIIII Batavorum
	Coh III Batavorum
	Coh III Nerviorum
	Coh IIII Gallorum (third century)
Great Chesters	Vex Raetorum Gaesatorum
	Coh Raetorum (mid-second century)
	Coh VI Nerviorum
	Coh II Asturum (early to mid-third century)
Carvoran	Coh I Hamiorum Sagittariorum (Hadrianic, late Antonine)
	Coh II Delmatarum
	Coh I Batavorum
	Numerus
Birdoswald	Coh I Aelia Dacorum (third century)
	Coh I Thracum C. R. (early third-century)
	Coh ? (late third century)
Castlesteads	Coh IIII Gallorum Equitata
	Coh II Tungrorum milliaria equitata C. L. (mid-third century)
	Equites
Burgh-by-Sands	Coh I Nervana Germanorum milliaria equitata
	Numerus Maurorum Aurelianorum (mid-third century)
Bowness-on-Solway	Coh? (mid-third century)
Birrens	Coh II Tungrorum milliaria equitata C. L. (Antonine)
	Coh I Nervana Germanorum milliaria equitata
Melandra Castle	Coh I Frisiavonum
Brough-on-Noe	Coh I Aquitanorum
Whitley Castle	Coh II Nerviorum

Appendix III:
Dated Building-Inscriptions from Forts in North-West England

A. Vespasian	Chester (A.D. 79)	*RIB* 463 & *EE* ix, 1039; *Britannia* I (1970), 292f.
B. Trajan	Chester (A.D. 102–17)	*RIB* 464
	Lancaster (A.D. 102–17)	*RIB* 604
	Melandra (A.D. 98–117)	*RIB* 208
C. Hadrian	Bowes (A.D. 130–3)	*RIB* 739
	Hardknott	*JRS* lv (1965), 222
	Moresby (A.D. 128–38)	*RIB* 801
	Maryport (A.D. 117–38)	*RIB* 851
	Netherby	*RIB* 974
	Bewcastle	*RIB* 995
	Great Chesters (A.D. 128–38)	*RIB* 1736
D. Antoninus Pius	Castlesteads (A.D. 140–4)	*RIB* 1997
	Birrens (A.D. 157–8)	*RIB* 2110
	Brough-on-Noe (A.D. 158)	*RIB* 283
E. Marcus Aurelius	Ribchester (A.D. 163–6)	*RIB* 589
	Hardknott (A.D. 163–6)	*RIB* 793
	Vindolanda (A.D. 163–6)	*RIB* 1703
	Great Chesters (A.D. 163–6)	*RIB* 1737
	Carvoran (A.D. 163–6)	*RIB* 1809
F. Septimius Severus	Chester (A.D. 194–6)	*RIB* 465
	Manchester	*RIB* 581
	Bainbridge (A.D. 205–8)	*RIB* 722, 723
	Greta Bridge (A.D. 205–8)	*RIB* 746
	Bowes (A.D. 205–8)	*RIB* 740
	Brough (A.D. 197)	*RIB* 757
	Birdoswald (A.D. 198–209)	*RIB* 1910
G. Caracalla	Maryport (A.D. 211–17)	*RIB* 832, 850
	Old Carlisle (A.D. 213)	*RIB* 928
	Netherby (A.D. 213)	*RIB* 976, 977
	Vindolanda (A.D. 213)	*RIB* 1705
	Birdoswald (A.D. 211–17)	*RIB* 1911
	Whitley Castle (A.D. 213 and 215–16)	*RIB* 1202, 1203
	Lancaster (?)	*Britannia* xvii (1986), 436

H. Elagabalus	Birdoswald (A.D. 219)	*RIB* 1914
I. Severus Alexander	Ribchester (A.D. 222–35)	*RIB* 587
	Old Penrith (A.D. 222–35)	*RIB* 919, 929
	Old Carlisle (A.D. 222–35)	*RIB* 929
	Netherby (A.D. 222)	*RIB* 978
	Vindolanda (A.D. 223)	*RIB* 1706
	Great Chesters (A.D. 225)	*RIB* 1738
J. Gordian III	Maryport (A.D. 238–44)	*RIB* 854
	Stanwix (A.D. 238–44)	*RIB* 2027
K. Postumus	Lancaster (A.D. 262–6)	*RIB* 605
L. Diocletian	Birdoswald (A.D. 297–305)	*RIB* 1912

Appendix IV:
Names of Roman Sites
in North-West England

The names by which Roman sites were known have proved extraordinarily elusive; relating known names to particular sites is hazardous, and confidence in such an exercise is not enhanced by the fact that new major sites continue to appear – for example, in recent years, Burgh I, Blennerhasset and Cummersdale – and speculation remains concerning the possible existence of other sites as yet unknown.

The most reliable evidence is that which derives from inscriptions found at the sites in question; in this way we can be virtually certain of five identifications – Ribchester/Bremetennacum, Chesterholm/Vindolanda, Birdoswald/Banna, Chester/Deva and Luguvalium/Carlisle. It further seems likely that on epigraphic grounds we can accept that Old Carlisle (Red Dial) was either Maglone or Magis. It has also been shown (by Hassall, 1976) that the sequence of forts at the western end of Hadrian's Wall can be at least partially reconstructed thus –

Bowness-on-Solway	Maia
Burgh-by-Sands	Aballava
Stanwix	Uxellodunum (though probably also called Petriana)
Castlesteads	Camboglanna
Birdoswald	Banna

The majority of other known names of Roman sites appear in three extant or partially-extant documents – the *Antonine Itinerary*, the *Notitia Dignitatum* and the *Ravenna Cosmography*. These present us with sequences or collections of names, which require interpretation before we can propose identifications for them; even then we have to admit that we have too small a number of

certainties to be able to offer reliable identifications in any but a few cases.

The Antonine Itinerary

This document, compiled in the early third century A.D., consists of lists of names, separated by distances and arranged in 'routes'. Roman sites in north-west England are found in Routes II, V and X. It should be noted that a fundamental problem attaches to interpretation: since the document was compiled early in the third century A.D., we should assume that sites which are named were occupied at the time of compilation. As we have seen, clear chronologies have as yet been established for only a few sites, leaving us in doubt in some cases whether they were in fact occupied at the relevant time.

Route X ran for 150 miles from Clanoventa to Mediolanum, traditionally Ravenglass to Whitchurch (in Shropshire). Intermediate points on the route are Galava, Alone, Galacum, Bremetonnacum, Coccium, Mamucium and Condate; of the nine sites, only Bremetonnacum can on epigraphic grounds be identified – that is, with Ribchester. There is no pressing reason to place the beginning of the route at Ravenglass; indeed there is a strong possibility in view of the dedication from Lancaster to the god, Ialonus, (possibly a river-deity) that Galava, Alone and Galacum should be taken as the names of sites on the river Lune – respectively Low Borrow Bridge (Galava), Burrow-in-Lonsdale (Alone) and Lancaster (Galacum). Clanoventa might then be suitably identified with Ambleside; the disposition and role of the fort (described in chapter 4) are well encapsulated in a name which means 'market by the clear water'. South of Ribchester, the route makes for

Manchester (Mamcunium) and Northwich (Condate), passing through Coccium; in view of recent work at Wigan, there is no difficulty in associating it with Coccium, although there is a view that Coccium might be a site as yet unknown – possibly in the Bolton area.

Route II ran for 481 miles from the northern frontier to the port of Richborough in Kent; it specifies initial stages from Blatobulgium and Castra Exploratorum to Luguvallum. Luguvallum (or Luguvalium) is to be identified with Carlisle, and the preceding sites of Netherby (Castra Exploratorum/Fort of the Scouts) and Birrens (Blatobulgium) seem well-founded. South of Carlisle, the route runs to Voreda, Brovonacae, Verterae, Lavatrae and then through Cataractone and Isurium to Eburacum. There is little doubt that the last three are Catterick, Aldborough and York, and that therefore the route crosses from west to east over Stainmore. The stated distances are consistent with stages from Carlisle to Old Penrith (Voreda), Kirkby Thore (Brovonacae), Brough (Verterae) and Bowes (Lavatrae).

Route V ran for 442 miles from London to Carlisle (Luguvalium); the latter portion of this route proceeds through York (Eburacum) and Aldborough (Isubrigantum) to Catterick (Cataractone), and thence to Bowes (Lavatrae) and Brough (Verterae). Thus far this route is identical to Route II – but in reverse. In Route V, however, there is no mention of Brovonacae (Kirkby Thore) or Voreda (Old Penrith); instead, Brocavum lies between Brough and Carlisle. The most suitable location for Brocavum is Brougham which like its medieval counterpart, stood at the important junction of the Stainmore and the north/south routes.

From the *Antonine Itinerary*, therefore, sixteen sites in north-west England can be associated with names with varying degrees of certainty.

The Notitia Dignitatum

Most of the problems raised by this document are too far-reaching for discussion in the present context; dating and purpose have been the subjects of much speculation, as have the identities of site-names and military units listed as belonging to the command of the officer known as the *Dux Britanniarum* (Duke of the Britains), who was based at York and controlled the northern frontier area. It is generally held that most of the information belongs to the second half of the fourth century, although that concerning the 'wall sub-section' may date from the previous century. At the same time, great problems are caused by the fact that, with the exception of the 'wall sub-section', the sites are not apparently listed in conformity with any geographical or military logic; further, there is some evidence of textual disturbance in the portion dealing with the western end of Hadrian's Wall.

The 'wall sub-section' contains some names familiar from the Rudge Cup, although there are problems of textual interpretation. It is reasonable to suppose that the western sequence includes Castlesteads (Amboglanna) and Stanwix (Uxellodunum/ Petrianae); however, the name (though not the military unit) of Birdoswald has been lost. Burgh-by-Sands appears as Aballaba, although there is no apparent listing of Drumburgh or Bowness-on-Solway. Beyond Aballaba, the names Congavata, Axelodunum, Gabrosentum, Tunnocelum and Glannibanta have been taken to be the forts of the Cumberland coast – Beckfoot, Maryport, Burrow Walls, Moresby and Ravenglass; of the military units mentioned in the Notitia list some are known from epigraphic evidence to have been garrisoned at coastal sites. For example, Cohors I Hispanorum is known at Maryport, whilst Cohors II Lingonum and Cohors II Thracum are both evidenced at Moresby. Further, a lead sealing of Cohors I Aelia Classica was found in the 1977/78 excavations at Ravenglass, and more recently a discharge-diploma of a soldier from the same unit.

It is possible in view of this that we could postulate identifications of Beckfoot/Congavata, Maryport/Axelodunum, Moresby/

Gabrosentum and Ravenglass/Tunnocelum. Glannibanta could then be identified with Ambleside (Clanoventa of the *Antonine Itinerary*). There is then no reason why Alione should not be Burrow-in-Lonsdale, particularly since the next site listed is Bremetenracum/Ribchester.

The Duke's list in the *Notitia* also includes Lavatrae, Verterae, and Braboniacum; these appear to preserve the sequence over Stainmore marked in the *Antonine Itinerary* of Bowes, Brough and Kirkby Thore. Moreover, the unit placed at Brough, the *numerus directorum* (or Unit of Dispatchers) would be appropriate for a site which has produced such a large and variable collection of lead sealings for official packages. Maglone and Magis are placed after Braboniacum and, as we have seen, there is some reason to suppose that one of these might be Old Carlisle.

This leaves unidentified Magis or Maglone, Longovicium (which appears at this point but which may be a north-eastern site), Derventio (often taken as Papcastle, which in view of its probable significance would be expected to have had a place in the list), and finally Olenacum and Virosidum (which could be Ilkley and Bainbridge). These postulated identifications do not restore total logic to the sequence in the Notitia, or solve all of the problems, but they do provide some geographical connections and sequences.

The Ravenna Cosmography

This document of the seventh century appears to derive in part from a road map; lists of names radiate from centres which are mentioned once and subsequently have to be understood at the commencement of each route for which they are the starting-point. Thus Manchester (Mautio) is the starting-point for four routes – to Alicuna (Ilkley), to Camulodunum (Slack?), and to Caluvio (Lancaster), whilst the fourth runs to Bresmetenacum Veteranorum (Ribchester) into West Yorkshire. Place-names are not necessarily listed on every route on which they feature. Thus Ribchester is not listed on the route leading from Manchester to Lancaster, but simply on that which heads into West Yorkshire.

Within the list that leads from Manchester, there appear to be subsidiary 'departure-points'; thus after Caluvio (Lancaster) came Galluvio (Low Borrow Bridge), Medibogdo, Cantiventi, Iuliocenon and Gabrocentio. Of these Medibogdo ('fort in the middle of a bow') would seem to be a strong description of Watercrook, and thus represents a fresh departure from Lancaster. It would appear to lead to Ambleside (Cantiventi, possibly, though not necessarily, to be identified with Clanoventa), and then to Iuliocenon (Tunnocelum, and probably Ravenglass) and Gabrocentio (Gabrosentum/Moresby). Alauna, which follows Gabrocentio, has usually been identified with Maryport, but might in fact represent a further departure from Lancaster along the Lune Valley, to Burrow-in-Lonsdale (Alauna). It has to be said that this leaves Bribra, Maio, Olerica, Derventio and Ravonia hard to identify, although Bribra might be Virosidum (Bainbridge), from which two routes lead – one into Yorkshire (To Malton/Derventio), the other to Kirkby Thore (probably to be identified with Ravonia).

Kirkby Thore then becomes a new departure-point: first, a route leads to Valteris (Brough), and then a second to Old Penrith (Bereda) and Carlisle (Lagubalium, close to the form found in Bede). A third then proceeds northwards to a new centre – Magnis (or Carvoran); from here one road leads to Gabaglanda (Castlesteads), another to Vindolanda. A subsequent starting-point is Banna (Birdoswald) leading first to Uxellodunum (possibly, as we have seen, an alternative name for Stanwix), Avalava (Burgh-by-Sands) and Maia (Bowness-on-Solway); a second route from Birdoswald leads to Fanum Cocidi, which was probably Bewcastle. Further south, the Cosmography listing provides a clear sequence of Deva Victrix (Chester) and Condate (Northwich).

Although much remains unclear, this short discussion indicates that there is room for re-arrangement and re-thinking of traditional identifications, although fresh certainty can be applied only with the discovery of new inscriptions and other documents (e.g. writing tablets) which can provide us with new firm identifications.

A word should finally be said about the site of Portus Setantiorum which figures in the Geography of Ptolemy of Alexandria. It is usually assumed that this represents a site that has been lost through coastal change and now lies off Fleetwood beneath the waters of the Lune Estuary. It is a story that readily lends itself to romantic embroidery. We should, however, bear in mind that the Setantii may have lived in southern Cumbria, and the Portus Setantiorum may be an elusive site near the southern end of Lake Windermere (Shotter, 1995a).

For further reading on the place-name evidence, see particularly –

Rivet, 1970 – *The Antonine Itinerary*

Goodburn and Bartholomew, 1976 – *The Notitia Dignitatum*

Richmond and Crawford, 1949 – *The Ravenna Cosmography*

Roman Site-Names in North-West England

Site	Epigraphic etc.	It. Ant.	Not. Dign.	Rav. Cosm.	Other
Ambleside		CLANOVENTA	GLANNIBANTA	CANTIVENTI	
Beckfoot			CONGAVATA		
Bewcastle				FANUM COCIDI	
Birdoswald	BANNA			BANNA	BANNA
Birrens		BLATOBULGIUM			
Blennerhasset					
Bowes		LAVATRAE	LAVATRES	LAVARIS	
Bowness				MAIA	MAIA
Brough		VERTERAE	VERTERAE	VALTERIS	
Brougham		BROCAVUM			
Burgh-by-Sands			ABALLABA	AVALAVA	ABALLABA
Burrow-in-Lonsdale	ALONE	ALIONE	ALAUNA		
Burrow Walls					
Caermote					
Carlisle	LUGUVALIUM	LUGUVALLUM		LAGUBALIUM	LUGUBALIA
Castleshaw					
Castlesteads			AMBOGLANNA	GABAGLANDA	CAMBOGLANS
Chester	DEVA			DEVA VICTRIX	
Cummersdale					
Drumburgh					
Hardknott					
Kirkbride	BRIGA(?)				
Kirkby Thore		BROVONACAE	BRABONIACUM	RAVONIA	
Kirkham					
Lancaster		GALACUM		CALUVIO	
Low Borrow Bridge		GALAVA			
Manchester		MAMUCIUM		MAUTIO	
Maryport				AXELODUNUM	
Moresby		GABROSENTUM	GABROCENTIO		
Netherby		CASTRA EXPLORATORUM			
Northwich		CONDATE		CONDATE	
Old Carlisle	MAGIS(?)		MAGIS(?)		
Old Penrith		VOREDA		BEREDA	
Papcastle			DERVENTIO(?)		
Ravenglass				TUNNOCELUM	IULIOCENON
Ribchester	BREMETENNACUM BREMETONNACUM		BREMETENRACUM	BRESNETENACUM VETERANORUM	
Stanwix			PETRIANAE		UXELODUM
Walton-le-Dale					
Watercrook				MEDIBOGDO	
Wigan		COCCIUM			
Wilderspool					

Bibliography

Austen, 1990: Austen P. S., *Bewcastle and Old Penrith*, Kendal

Barker, 1975: Barker P., Excavations at the Baths Basilica at Wroxeter 1966–74, *Britannia* VI, 106–17

Bellhouse, 1953: Bellhouse R. L., A Roman Fort at Wreay Hall, near Carlisle, CW² LIII, 49–51

Bellhouse, 1954a: Bellhouse R. L., A newly-discovered Roman Fort at Park House, near Carlisle, CW² LIV, 9–16

Bellhouse, 1954b: Bellhouse R. L., Roman Sites on the Cumberland Coast, 1954, CW² LIV, 28–55

Bellhouse, 1955: Bellhouse R. L., The Roman Fort at Burrow Walls, near Workington, CW² LV, 30–45

Bellhouse, 1960a: Bellhouse R. L., The Roman Forts near Caermote, CW² LX, 20–3

Bellhouse, 1960b: Bellhouse R. L., Excavations in Eskdale, the Muncaster Roman Kilns, CW² LX, 1–12

Bellhouse, 1967: Bellhouse R. L., The Aughertree Fell Enclosures, CW² LXVII, 26–30

Bellhouse, 1971: Bellhouse R. L., Roman Tileries at Scalesceugh and Brampton, CW² LXXI, 35–44

Bellhouse, 1981: Bellhouse R. L., Hadrian's Wall: The Limiting Ditches in the Cardurnock Peninsular, *Britannia* XII, 135–42

Bellhouse, 1989: Bellhouse R. L., *Roman Sites on the Cumberland Coast*, Kendal

Bellhouse, 1992: Bellhouse R. L., *Joseph Robinson of Maryport: Archaeologist Extraordinary*, Ilkley

Bellhouse and Richardson, 1982: Bellhouse R. L. and Richardson G. G. S., The Trajanic Fort at Kirkbride; the terminus of the Stanegate Frontier, CW² LXXXII, 35–50

Birley, 1973: Birley A. R., Petillius Cerialis and the Conquest of Brigantia, *Britannia* IV, 179–90

Birley, 1975: Birley A. R., Agricola, the Flavian Dynasty and Tacitus, pp. 139–54 in Levick B. (ed.), *The Ancient Historian and his Materials*, Farnborough (Hants)

Birley, 1932: Birley E. B., Materials for the History of Roman Brougham, CW² XXXII, 124–39

Birley, 1946: Birley E. B., The Roman Site at Burrow-in-Lonsdale, CW² XLVI, 126–56

Birley, 1947: Birley E. B., The Roman Fort at Low Borrow Bridge, CW² XLVII, 1–19

Birley, 1951: Birley E. B., The Roman Fort and Settlement at Old Carlisle, CW² LI, 16–39

Birley, 1953: Birley E. B., The Roman Milestone at Middleton-in-Lonsdale, CW² LIII, 52–62

Birley, 1958: Birley E. B., The Roman Fort at Brough-under-Stainmore, CW² LVIII, 31–56

Birley, 1961: Birley E. B., *Research on Hadrian's Wall*, Kendal

Birley, 1963: Birley E. B., Roman Papcastle, CW² LXIII, 96–125

Birley, 1977: Birley R. E., *Vindolanda: A Roman Frontier Post on Hadrian's Wall*, London

Birley, Birley and Birley, 1993: Birley E. B., Birley R. E. and Birley A. R., *Vindolanda II: The Early Wooden Forts*, Hexham

Blake, 1959: Blake B., Excavations of Native (Iron Age) Sites in Cumberland, 1956–58, CW² LIX, 1–14

Bowman and Thomas, 1983: Bowman A. K. and Thomas J. D., *Vindolanda: The Latin Writing Tablets. Britannia Monographs* 4, London

Branigan, 1980: Branigan K., Villas in the North: Change in the Rural Landscape, pp. 18–27 in Branigan K. (ed.) *Rome and the Brigantes*, Sheffield

Braund, 1984: Braund D., Some Observations on Cartimandua, *Britannia* XV, 1–6

Breeze, 1975: Breeze D. J., The Abandonment of the Antonine Wall: its Date and Implications, *Scot. Arch. Forum* VII, 67–78

Breeze, 1982: Breeze D. J., *The Northern Frontiers of Roman Britain*, London

Breeze, 1988: Breeze D. J., The Roman Army in Cumbria, CW² LXXXVIII, 9–22

Breeze and Dobson, 1976: Breeze D. J. and Dobson B., *Hadrian's Wall*, London

Bruton, 1908: Bruton F. A., *Excavation of the Roman Forts at Castleshaw*, Manchester

Bruton, 1909: Bruton F. A., *The Roman Fort at Manchester*, Manchester

Buxton, 1996: Buxton K. M., Roman Ribchester, pp. 11–18 in Graystone P., *Walking Roman Roads in the Fylde and the Ribble Valley*, Lancaster

Buxton and Howard-Davis, forthcoming: Buxton K. M. and Howard-Davis C. L. E., *Excavations on the Site of the Roman fort at Dowbridge, Kirkham, 1994*, Lancaster

Charlesworth, 1964: Charlesworth D., Recent Work at Kirkby Thore, CW² LXIV, 61–75

Charlesworth, 1965: Charlesworth D., Excavations at Papcastle 1961–62, CW² LXV, 102–14

Clare, 1989: Clare T., The Prehistoric Landscape, pp. 9–27 in Rollinson W. (ed.), *The Lake District: Landscape Heritage*, Newton Abbot

Collingwood, 1931: Collingwood R. G., A Roman Fortlet on Barrock Fell, near Low Hesket, CW² XXXI, 111–18

Collingwood, 1908–9: Collingwood W. G., Report on an Exploration of the Romano-British Settlement at Ewe Close, CW² IX, 295–309

Davies, 1971: Davies R. W., The Roman Military Diet, *Britannia* II, 122–42

Davies, 1977: Davies R. W., Cohors I Hispanorum and the Garrisons of Maryport, CW² LXXVII, 7–16

Edwards, 1971: Edwards B. J. N., Roman Finds from Contrebis, CW² LXXI, 17–34

Edwards, 1972: Edwards B. J. N., *Ribchester*, National Trust Handbook

Edwards, 1992: Edwards B. J. N., *The Ribchester Hoard*, Preston

Edwards and Webster, 1985–8: Edwards B. J. N. and Webster P. V., *Ribchester Excavations*, Cardiff

Evans and Scull, 1990: Evans J. and Scull C., Fieldwork on the Roman Fort site at Blennerhasset, Cumbria, CW² XC, 127–38

Ferrill, 1991: Ferrill A., *Roman Imperial Grand Strategy*, Lanham

Gibbons, 1989: Gibbons P., Excavations and Observations at Kirkby Thore, CW² LXXXIX, 93–130

Gillam, 1949: Gillam J. P., Also, Along the Line of the Wall, CW² XLIX, 38–58

Gillam, 1958: Gillam J. P., Roman and Native, 122–197, pp. 60–90 in Richmond I. A. (ed.), *Roman and Native in North Britain*, Edinburgh

Gillam, Jobey and Welsby, 1993: Gillam J. P., Jobey I. M. and Welsby D. A., *The Roman Bath-house at Bewcastle, Cumbria*, Kendal

Goodburn and Bartholomew, 1976: Goodburn R. and Bartholomew P. (eds), *Aspects of the Notitia Dignitatum*, Oxford (BAR 15)

Graystone, 1992: Graystone P., *Walking Roman Roads in Bowland*, Lancaster

Hanson *et al.*, 1979: Hanson W. S., with Daniels C. M., Dore J. N. and Gillam J. P., The Agricolan Supply-base at Red House, Corbridge, *Arch. Ael.*⁵ VII, 1–88

Hanson, 1987: Hanson W. S., *Agricola and the Conquest of the North*, London

Hanson and Campbell, 1986: Hanson W. S. and Campbell D. B., The Brigantes: From Clientage to Conquest, *Britannia* XVII, 73–89

Hanson and Maxwell, 1983: Hanson W. S. and Maxwell G., *The Antonine Wall: Rome's North-West Frontier*, Edinburgh

Hartley, 1966: Hartley B. R., Some Problems of the Roman Military Occupation of Northern England, *Northern History* I, 7–10

Hartley, 1972: Hartley B. R., The Roman Occupations of Scotland: the Evidence of Samian Ware, *Britannia* III, 1–55

Hartley, 1980: Hartley B. R., The Brigantes and the Roman Army, pp. 2–7 in Branigan K. (ed), *Rome and the Brigantes*, Sheffield

Haselgrove, 1997: Haselgrove C., The Iron Age, pp. 61–74 in Newman R. (ed.), *The Archaeology of Lancashire*, Lancaster

Hartley and Webster, 1973: Hartley K. F. and Webster P. V., Romano-British Pottery Kilns near Wilderspool, *Arch. Journ.* CXXX, 77–103

Hassall, 1976: Hassall M. W. C., Britain in the Notitia, pp. 103–117 in Goodburn R. and Bartholomew P. (eds), *vide supra*

Henig, 1984: Henig M., *Religion in Roman Britain*, London

Heurgon, 1951: Heurgon J., The Amiens Patera, *JRS* XLI, 22–4

Higham, 1978: Higham N. J., Early Field Survival in North Cumbria, pp. 119–25 in Bowen

H. C. and Fowler P. J. (eds), *Early Land Allotment in the British Isles*, Oxford (*BAR* 48)

Higham, 1979: Higham N. J., An Aerial Survey of the Upper Lune Valley, pp. 31–8 in Higham N. J. (ed.), *The Changing Past*, Manchester

Higham, 1980: Higham N. J., Native Settlements West of the Pennines, pp. 41–7 in Branigan K. (ed.), *Rome and the Brigantes*, Sheffield

Higham, 1982: Higham N. J., 'Native' Settlements on the North Slopes of the Lake District, *CW*² LXXXII, 29–33

Higham, 1986: Higham N. J., *The Northern Counties to A.D. 1000*, London

Higham and Jones, 1975: Higham N. J. and Jones G. D. B., Frontier, Forts and Farmers, *Arch. Journ.* CXXXII, 16–53

Higham and Jones, 1985: Higham N. J. and Jones G. D. B., *The Carvetii*, Gloucester

Hildyard, 1951: Hildyard E. J. W., Renewed Excavation at Low Borrow Bridge, *CW*² LI, 40–66

Hildyard, 1954: Hildyard E. J. W., Excavations at Burrow-in-Lonsdale, *CW*² LIV, 66–101

Hill, 1970: Hill P. V., *The Dating and Arrangement of Undated Coins of Rome, A.D. 98–148*, London

Hinchliffe and Williams, 1992: Hinchliffe J. and Williams J. H., *Roman Warrington*, Manchester

Hind, 1977: Hind J. G. F., The 'Genounian' Part of Britain, *Britannia* VIII, 229–34

Hind, 1983: Hind J. G. F., Who betrayed Britain to the Barbarians in A.D. 367? *Northern History* XIX, 1–7

Hobley, 1989: Hobley A. S., The Numismatic Evidence for the post-Agricolan abandonment of the Roman Frontier in Northern Scotland, *Britannia* XX, 69–74

Hogg, 1965: Hogg R., Excavation of the Roman Auxiliary tilery, Brampton, *CW*² LXV, 133–68

Jarrett, 1976: Jarrett M. G., *Maryport, Cumbria: A Roman Fort and its Garrison*, Kendal

Johnson, 1980: Johnson A. S., *Later Roman Britain*, London

Jones and Price, 1985: Jones G. C. and Price J., Excavations at the Wiend, Wigan, 1982–84, *GMAJ* I, 25–33

Jones, 1968: Jones G. D. B., The Romans in the North West, *Northern History* III, 1–26

Jones, 1970: Jones G. D. B., Roman Lancashire, *Arch. Journ.* CXXVII, 237–45

Jones, 1972: Jones G. D. B., Excavations at Northwich (Condate), *Arch. Journ.* CXXVIII, 31–77

Jones, 1974: Jones G. D. B., *Roman Manchester*, Altrincham

Jones, 1975: Jones G. D. B., The North-Western Interface, pp. 93–106 in Fowler P. J. (ed), *Recent work in Rural Archaeology*, Bradford-on-Avon

Jones, 1979: Jones G. D. B., The Future of Aerial Photography in the North, pp. 75–87 in Higham N. J. (ed.), *The Changing Past*, Manchester

Jones, 1980: Jones G. D. B., Archaeology and Coastal Change in the North-West, pp. 87–102 in Thompson F. H. (ed.), *Archaeology and Coastal Change*, London

Jones, 1982: Jones G. D. B., The Solway Frontier: Interim Report 1976–81, *Britannia* XIII, 284–97

Jones, 1990: Jones G. D. B., The Emergence of the Tyne-Solway Frontier, pp. 98–107 in Maxfield V. A. and Dobson M. J. (eds), *Roman Frontier Studies, 1989*, Exeter

Jones, 1991: Jones G. D. B., Farndon: An Archaeological Opportunity, *MAB* VI, 75–7

Jones, 1993: Jones G. D. B., Excavations on a Coastal Tower, Hadrian's Wall: Campfield Tower 2B, Bowness-on-Solway, *MAB* VIII, 31–9

Jones, 1994/5: Jones G. D. B., Farnhill: Excavation on the Solway Frontier, *MAB* IX, 23–7

Jones and Shotter, 1988: Jones G. D. B. and Shotter D. C. A., *Roman Lancaster*, Manchester

Jones and Webster, 1968: Jones G. D. B. and Webster P. V., Mediolanum: Excavations at Whitchurch, 1965–6, *Arch. Journ.* CXXV, 193–254

Jones and Wild, 1970: Jones G. D. B. and Wild J. P., Manchester University Excavations at Brough-on-Noe (*Navio*), 1969, *Derbys. Arch. Journ.* LXX, 99–106

Jones, 1975: Jones M. J., *Roman Fort-Defences to A.D. 117*, Oxford (*BAR* 21)

Jones, 1977: Jones M. J., Archaeological Work

at Brough-under-Stainmore 1971–72: I, The Roman Discoveries, *CW*[2] LXXVII, 35–50

Jones, 1981: Jones R. F. J., Change in the Frontier, Northern Britain in the Third Century, pp. 393–414 in King A. and Henig M. (eds) *The Roman West in the Third Century*, Oxford (*BAR* (S) 109)

Keppie and Walker, 1981: Keppie L. J. F. and Walker J. J., Fortlets on the Antonine Wall at Seabegs Wood, Kinneil and Cleddans, *Britannia* XII, 143–62

Kilbride-Jones, 1938: Kilbride-Jones H. E., Excavation of a Native Settlement at Milking Gap, High Shield, Northumberland, *Arch. Ael.*[4] XV, 303–50

King, 1970: King A., Romano-British Metalwork from the Settle District of West Yorkshire, *YAJ* XLII, 410–17

King, 1978: King A., Gauber High Pasture, Ribblehead – an interim report, pp. 21–5 in Hall R. A. (ed.), *Viking Age York and the North*, (CBA Research Report 27), London

Lambert *et al* 1996: Lambert J., with Hair N., Howard-Davis C. L. E., Newman R. and Oliver T., *Transect through Time*, Lancaster

Leather and Webster, 1988: Leather G. M. and Webster P. V., The Quernmore Kilns, pp. 85–93 in Jones G. D. B. and Shotter D. C. A. (eds), *Roman Lancaster*, Manchester

Leech, 1993: Leech R. H., The Roman Fort and *vicus* at Ambleside: Archaeological Research in 1982, *CW*[2] XCIII, 51–74

Lowndes, 1963: Lowndes R. A. C., 'Celtic' fields, farms and burial mounds in the Lune Valley, *CW*[2] LXIII, 77–95

Lowndes, 1964: Lowndes R. A. C., Excavation of a Romano-British Farmstead at Eller Beck, *CW*[2] LXIV, 1–13

Mann, 1974: Mann J. C., The Northern Frontier after A.D. 369, *Glasgow Arch. Journ.* III, 34–42

Mann and Dunwell, 1995: Mann S. and Dunwell A., An interim note on further discoveries in the Roman *vicus* at Ambleside, 1992–93, *CW*[2] XCV, 79–83

Manning, 1975: Manning W. H., Economic influences on land use in the military areas of the Highland Zone during the Roman period, pp. 112–6 in Evans J. G., Limbrey S. and Cleere H. (eds) *The Effect of Man on the Landscape: the Highland Zone* (CBA Research Report 11), London

Maxwell, 1990: Maxwell G., *A Battle Lost*, Edinburgh

McCarthy, 1980: McCarthy M. R., *Carlisle, A Frontier City*, Carlisle

McCarthy, 1990: McCarthy M. R., *A Roman, Anglian and Medieval Site at Blackfriars Street, Carlisle*, Kendal

McCarthy, 1991: McCarthy M. R., *Roman Waterlogged Remains at Castle Street, Carlisle*, Kendal

McCarthy, 1993: McCarthy M. R., *Carlisle: History and Guide*, Stroud

McPeake, 1978: McPeake J. C., The First Century A. D., pp. 9–16 in Strickland T. J. and Davey P. J. (eds), *New Evidence for Roman Chester*, Liverpool

Miller, 1975: Miller M., Stilicho's Pictish War, *Britannia* VI, 141–5

Millet, 1990: Millet M., *The Romanisation of Britain*, Cambridge

Newman, 1997: Newman R. (ed.), *The Archaeology of Lancashire*, Lancaster

Penney and Shotter, 1996: Penney S. H. and Shotter D. C. A., An Inscribed Roman Salt-pan from Shavington, Cheshire, *Britannia* XXVII, 360–5

Pennington, 1970: Pennington W., Vegetation History in the North-West of England: a regional synthesis, pp. 41–79 in Walker D. and West R. G. (eds), *Studies in the Vegetational History of the British Isles*, Cambridge

Potter, 1977: Potter T. W. J., The Biglands Milefortlet and the Cumberland Coast Defences, *Britannia* VIII, 149–83

Potter, 1979: Potter T. W. J., *The Romans in North-West England*, Kendal

Poulter, 1982: Poulter A., Old Penrith: Excavations 1977 and 1979, *CW*[2] LXXXII, 51–66

Richardson, 1982: Richardson A., Evidence for Centuriation in the Inglewood Forest, *CW*[2] LXXXII, 67–71

Richardson, 1977: Richardson G. G. S., A Romano-British Farmstead at Fingland, *CW*[2] LXXVII, 53–9

Richardson and Richardson, 1980: Richardson G. G. S. and Richardson A., A Possible

Roman Road in the Kirkstone Pass and Matterdale, *CW*[2] LXXX, 160–2

Richmond, 1933: Richmond I. A., Castlefolds by Great Asby, *CW*[2] XXXIII, 233–7

Richmond, 1935: Richmond I. A., The Rudge Cup: II. The Inscription, *Arch. Ael.*[4] XII, 334–42

Richmond, 1936: Richmond I. A., Roman Leaden-Sealings from Brough-under-Stainmore, *CW*[2] XXXVI, 104–25

Richmond, 1945: Richmond I. A., The Sarmatae, Bremetenacum Veteranorum and the Regio Bremetennacensis, *JRS* XXXV, 15–29

Richmond, 1951: Richmond I. A., A Roman Arterial Signalling System in the Stainmore Pass, pp. 293–302 in Grimes W. F. (ed.), *Aspects of Archaeology in Britain and Beyond*, London

Richmond, 1954: Richmond I. A., Queen Cartimandua, *JRS* XLIV, 43–52

Richmond and Crawford, 1949: Richmond I. A. and Crawford O. G. S., The British Section of the Ravenna Cosmography. *Archaeologia* XCIII, 1–50

Richmond and McIntyre, 1934: Richmond I. A. and McIntyre J., The Roman Camps at Rey Cross and Crackenthorpe, *CW*[2] XXXIV, 50–61

Richmond and Steer, 1957: Richmond I. A. and Steer K. A., Castellum Veluniate and Civilians on a Roman Frontier, *PSAS* XC, 1–6

Rivet, 1970: Rivet A. L. F., The British Section of the Antonine Itinerary, *Britannia* I, 34–82

Robertson, 1973: Robertson A. S., *The Antonine Wall*, Glasgow

Robertson, 1974: Robertson A. S., Romano-British Coin Hoards, pp. 12–36 in Casey P. J. and Reece R. (eds), *Coins and the Archaeologist*, Oxford (*BAR 4*)

St. Joseph, 1951: St. Joseph J. K. S., Air Reconnaissance of North Britain, *JRS* XLI, 52–65

Salway, 1980: Salway P., The Vici: Urbanisation in the North, pp. 8–17 in Branigan K. (ed.), *Rome and the Brigantes*, Sheffield

Salway, 1981: Salway P., *Roman Britain*, Oxford

Shotter, 1973a: Shotter D. C. A., *Romans in Lancashire*, Clapham

Shotter, 1973b: Shotter D. C. A., Numeri Barca-riorum: A Note on RIB 601, *Britannia* IV, 206–9

Shotter, 1976: Shotter D. C. A., Coin Evidence and the Northern Frontier in the Second Century A. D., *PSAS* CVII, 81–91

Shotter, 1978a: Shotter D. C. A., Roman Coins from Carlisle, *CW*[2] LXXVIII, 201–3

Shotter, 1978b: Shotter D. C. A., Three Early Imperial Hoards from Lancashire, *Coin Hoards* IV, 44–5

Shotter, 1979: Shotter D. C. A., The Evidence of Coin-Loss and the Roman Occupation of North-West England, pp. 1–13 in Higham N. J. (ed.), *The Changing Past*, Manchester

Shotter, 1980: Shotter D. C. A., Roman Coins from Starling Castle, *CW*[2] LXXX, 163

Shotter, 1983: Shotter D. C. A., A Note on Tiles found on the Mitre Yard, Lancaster in 1973, *Britannia* XIV, 270–1

Shotter, 1989: Shotter D. C. A., Roman Coin-finds in Cumbria, *CW*[2] LXXXIX, 41–50

Shotter, 1990: Shotter D. C. A., *Roman Coins from North-West England*, Lancaster

Shotter, 1994: Shotter D. C. A., Rome and the Brigantes: Early Hostilities, *CW*[2] XCIV, 21–34

Shotter, 1995a: Shotter D. C. A., Romans in South Cumbria, *CW*[2] XCV, 73–7

Shotter, 1995b: Shotter D. C. A., *Roman Coins from North-West England: First Supplement*, Lancaster

Shotter, 1996: Shotter D. C. A., *The Roman Frontier in Britain*, Preston

Shotter and White, 1990: Shotter D. C. A. and White A. J., *The Roman Fort and Town of Lancaster*, Lancaster

Shotter and White, 1995: Shotter D. C. A. and White A. J., *The Romans in Lunesdale*, Lancaster

Simpson and Hodgson, 1947: Simpson F. G. and Hodgson K. S., The Coastal Milefortlet at Cardurnock, *CW*[2] XLVII, 78–127

Smith, 1959: Smith D. J., A Palmyrene Sculptor from South Shields, *Arch. Ael.*[4] XXXVII, 203–10

Southworth, 1989: Southworth J., *Walking Roman Roads in Cumbria*, Hale

Speidel, 1987: Speidel M. P., The Chattan War, the Brigantian Revolt and the Loss of the Antonine Wall, *Britannia* XVIII, 233–7

Start, 1985: Start D., Survey and Conservation Work at Castleshaw Roman Forts, 1984–5, *GMAJ* I, 13–18

Strickland, 1995: Strickland T. J., *The Romans at Wilderspool*, Warrington

Strickland and Davey, 1978: Strickland T. J. and Davey P. J. (eds), *New Evidence for Roman Chester*, Liverpool

Thompson, 1965: Thompson F. H., *Roman Cheshire*, Chester

Thompson, 1976: Thompson F. H., The Excavation of the Roman Amphitheatre of Chester, *Archaeologia* CV, 127–239

Thompson, 1980: Thompson F. H. (ed.), *Archaeology and Coastal Change*, London

Tindall, 1985: Tindall A. S., Wigan: The Development of the Town, *GMAJ* I, 19–23

Tylecote, 1962: Tylecote R. F., *Metallurgy in Archaeology*, London

Walker, 1989: Walker J. (ed.), *Castleshaw: The Archaeology of a Roman Fortlet*, Manchester

Ward, 1973: Ward J. H., The British Sections of the Notitia Dignitatum: an alternative interpretation, *Britannia* IV, 253–63

Webster, 1970: Webster G., *The Roman Imperial Army*, London

Webster, 1986: Webster G., *The British Celts and Their Gods under Rome*, London

Webster, 1975: Webster P. V., The Later Roman Occupation at Wilderspool, *CAJ* LVIII, 91–2

Wilkes, 1965: Wilkes J. J., Early Fourth-Century Rebuilding in Hadrian's Wall Forts, pp. 114–38 in Jarrett M. G. and Dobson B. (eds), *Britain and Rome*, Kendal

Woolliscroft, 1988: Woolliscroft D. J., The Outpost System of Hadrian's Wall, CW^2 LXXXVIII, 23–28

Woolliscroft and Swain, 1991: Woolliscroft D. J. and Swain S. A. M., The Roman "Signal" Tower at Johnson's Plain, CW^2 XCI, 19–29.